GREAT WALKS

THE PENNINE WAY

GREAT WALKS

THE PENNINE WAY

FRANK DUERDEN

Photography by David Ward

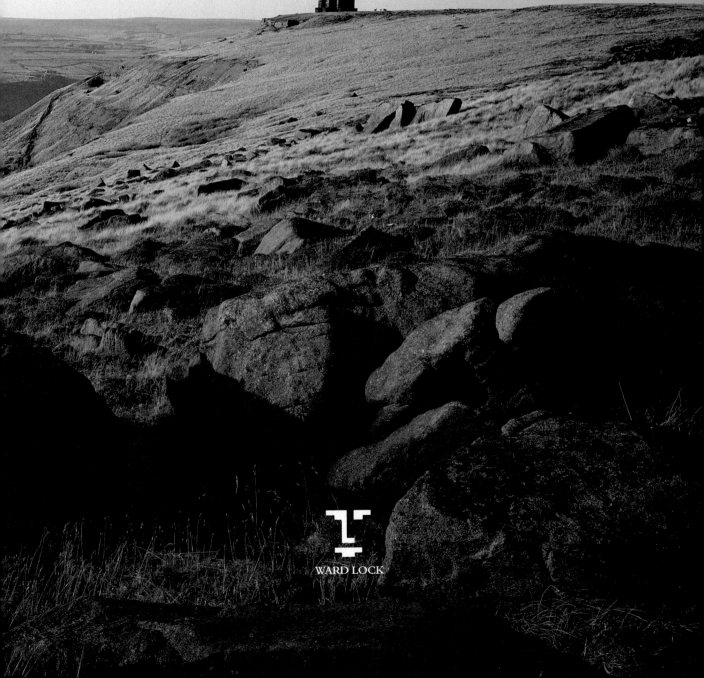

WARD LOCK

To Harold Smith,
who introduced me many years ago to the
moorlands of the central Pennines

© Text and maps Frank Duerden 1990
© Photographs and illustrations Ward Lock Limited
1990

First published in Great Britain in 1990
by Ward Lock Limited, Artillery House,
Artillery Row, London SW1P 1RT,
a Cassell Company

Designed by Jervis Tuttell

Text filmset in Perpetua
by M & R Typesetting

Printed and bound in Portugal
by Resopal

British Library Cataloguing in Publication Data
Duerden, Frank

Great Walks, the Pennine Way.
 1, England. Pennines. Long-distance footpaths: Pennine
Way. Description & travel
I. Title
796.5'1'09428

ISBN 0 7063 6813 4

Front page: Nichol Chair, High Cup (Day 12)
Previous page: Stoodley Pike (Day 3)

CONTENTS

ACKNOWLEDGMENTS

I must acknowledge my debt to so many people who have helped me during the preparation of this book. The walking of the Way, the research and finally the writing were all made easier and more enjoyable because of them.

In particular, I must thank the staff of the Countryside Commission: Roy Hickey (Countryside Officer — Recreation and Access) and Bob Monks (Mapping and Charting Officer) for information on the history of the Way, its maintenance and its route, and Eleanor Stevenson (Library) for help in locating various books and documents; the staff of the Ramblers' Association: Andrew Dalby (Secretary), Susan Larcombe (Personal Assistant) and their colleagues, for help with the section on Tom Stephenson; and Tom Scott Burns for information on drovers. The short extract from a publication is reproduced by permission of the Ramblers' Association; two short extracts were also taken from William Wilberforce's *Journey to the Lake District from Cambridge 1779*, published by Oriel Press.

As always my wife, Audrey, gave me great support and, in particular, helped me with the unenviable — but essential — task of proof reading. As he has done for other books in this series, David Ward has produced superb photographs; they do full justice to the glory of the Way. Finally, I would like to thank all the people I met during my journeys up the Pennine Way. In a few cases I met them again later and firm friendships developed. Generally, however, we were ships in the night. Nevertheless, their passing lights left a warming and lasting glow.

INTRODUCTION

In 1935 Tom Stephenson proposed the creation of a walkers' trail along the length of the Pennines and the Cheviot Hills from Edale in Derbyshire to the Scottish border. At that time it was a bold and imaginative concept. Over 70 miles (113 km) of new footpath would be required, some over moorland areas from which the public were firmly excluded. There was no practicable mechanism for creating the path or for obtaining the necessary access, nor, was there any will on the part of the government or other authorities to create such a path.

It is scarcely surprising, therefore, that it took thirty years—and World War II, with all its profound social and political implications—before the Pennine Way became a reality. Its opening on 24 April 1965 was a tribute, not just to the foresight and determination of Tom Stephenson, but also to his hard work and that of a host of others in the Ramblers' Association and related groups.

In the years since its official opening, the Pennine Way has been walked by thousands of people—either in one journey or in sections over a number of years—and there are thousands more who would walk it given half a chance. It is still very common to hear walkers say that the Way is their ultimate ambition, something to be done when there is the leisure time for it. Among the general public it is better known than any other long distance footpath. In every way, surely, it must have lived up to Tom Stephenson's hopes.

Yet the Way has been the subject of a fair amount of adverse comment, particularly in recent years. For example, the impression is given that it is a trail of mud from beginning to end, that you can follow the route by the litter, or that it is so overcrowded that the solitude which was claimed for it is now a thing of the past.

I disagree with all these views. As far as erosion is concerned, what is certainly true is that in some parts, particularly where the Way crosses blanket peat, surface damage is worrying and remedial steps are being taken. So often these areas, however, are popular in their own right and the Way merely adds to the traffic through them. Paths on Pen-y-ghent used by the Way have become badly eroded, but no more so than those on neighbouring Ingleborough or Whernside, which are not on the Way. At the moment there are very long stretches where erosion is not a problem. To the question 'Is the Pennine Way so badly eroded that for most people the pleasure of walking it is seriously reduced?', the answer must be an emphatic 'No!'. The question of litter can be dismissed out of hand; with the exception of some 'honey pots', it is not a particular problem and is no worse than in the countryside generally.

Surveys (see page 162) indicate that walking the Pennine Way is growing in popularity. However, those walking its entire length are still surprisingly few in number, although there are others who walk part of the way only and there are some areas, Malham, for example, where visitors are very numerous. Yet the overwhelming impression gained from the Way is still of peace and solitude. A meeting with other walkers is the opportunity for a few words and the exchange of news, rather than an unwelcome intrusion.

Without any doubt the Pennine Way is a great walk. Could any route designed by men of the calibre of Tom Stephenson, which goes through three National Parks and the largest Area of Outstanding Natural Beauty (which many think should have been given National Park status)—and deliberately seeks out some of the gems of those areas—be anything less? If it is, then the word 'great' no longer has any meaning. What can be conceded—perhaps—is that the task of walking for day after day can mask *at the time* the great merits of the individual sections. However, a little sober reflection afterwards should give a more balanced perspective. Thorough enjoyment is the typical experience of those who have walked the Way.

The journey will take you through some magnificent and varied scenery. From the harsh gritstone moorlands of Kinder to the gentle pastures of Craven, from the 'shapeless swell' of Stainmore to the shapely peak of Pen-y-ghent, from the busy valleys of the West Riding, where the industrial revolution was born, to the quiet uplands of the northern Pennines. You will follow old ways, now little frequented, but once busy with packhorse trains or drove herds; cross lonely stretches of moorland and visit dales of heart-catching beauty. You will climb hillside cloughs, cloaked in the final remnants of ancient woodland, and traverse areas of man-made forest; follow the grassy banks of rivers and the towpaths of famous trans-Pennine canals. The Way crosses clapper bridges, old packhorse bridges worn by use over many centuries, and wide two- or three-arched bridges built to accommodate the traffic of a later age; there are castles at Bowes and Thirlwall, weavers' cottages in the Hebden Valley, famous hostelries such as Tan Hill Inn, Pennine 'longhouses' and lonely bothies.

The past still hangs heavily on the Pennines and the spirits of those who made their mark there still linger; travellers along the Way who have imagination will feel their constant presence:

peoples of the Stone, Bronze and Iron Ages, hardened veterans of II Legion Augusta, Anglo-Saxon and Viking settlers, plaid-wrapped Scottish drovers, tough packmen, coal and lead miners, and mosstroopers coming quietly through the Border hills. Also the immortals: the travellers Daniel Defoe, Celia Fiennes and William Wilberforce; the Brontë sisters at Haworth, Charles Darwin at Malham Tarn House, Sir Walter Scott at Stainmore and Charles Dickens at Bowes enquiring into the conditions in Victorian schools for his novel *Nicholas Nickleby*.

With average luck on a summer journey you should have warm, dry days when the sun shines out of cloudless blue skies, when the miles seem short and the packs light; equally, there will be days of chilling rain, overcast skies and bitter winds. In winter, conditions can be severe, presenting a formidable challenge to even the hardiest of walkers.

This book is not a 'step-by-step' guide to the Way. It is intended firstly for those who have already walked the Way and wish to revive happy memories and widen their knowledge of it; and secondly for those who have not yet walked it but wish to get an idea of what the experience is like and to have the necessary information for planning their journey. The first part of the book is a description of the Way based on a journey of nineteen days, and the second part is concerned with logistics.

The Pennine Way can be a hard trudge or a glorious adventure. Your choice of companions, the vagaries of Pennine weather and the fickleness of the gods will no doubt all play a part; but in the end it is the hours of careful planning and preparation that are more likely to prove the deciding factors. Although 'in this world fast runners do not always win the race, and the brave do not always win the battle . . .', in practice, they usually do.

The Making of the Way

The history of the Pennine Way began modestly in 1935 with a letter from two American girls to the rambling and open-air correspondent of the *Daily Herald*, Tom Stephenson. Having already walked along part of the Appalachian Trail, a 2000-mile (3219 km) route from Georgia to Maine down the eastern seaboard of the United States established some four years earlier, they were looking for something similar which would occupy a walking holiday in Britain. The result was the article 'Wanted—A Long Green Trail', which appeared in the newspaper on 22 June.

Stephenson deplored the fact that, despite the great popularity of walking, no long distance trails comparable to the

Appalachian Trail existed in Britain. He therefore suggested the creation of one along the length of the Pennines from Edale to the Cheviots and outlined a possible route. It would be 'a meandering way . . . to include the best of that long range of moor and fell . . .', a 'through route to health and happiness for this and succeeding generations who may thus make acquaintance with some of the finest scenery in the land'.

This suggestion received an enthusiastic welcome from the walking fraternity and on 26–27 February 1938 a Pennine Way Association was formed at a special conference held at the Workers' Travel Association Guest House at Hope, Derbyshire, with Tom Stephenson and Edwin Royce as Joint Secretaries, Mrs H. Beaufoy as Assistant Secretary and a committee of six. The organization had as its aim, to survey the route in detail and to act as a pressure group to ensure its creation. The initial survey, carried out by local groups, revealed that nearly 70 miles (113 km) of new footpath would have to be created out of a total of about 250 miles (402 km), of which about 60 miles (97 km) would be over rough moorland and 10 miles (16 km) over pasture. This route was substantially the same as the one finally adopted, although there were differences in several areas.

Despite its reception, it was clear that formidable difficulties lay in the way of this proposal, particularly with regard to the creation of the missing sections of the route. The areas over which these would run were privately owned and in some cases jealously guarded by their owners. It is true that a mechanism for providing access to these areas was enshrined in the Access to Mountains Act introduced by Arthur Creech Jones as a Private Member's Bill in 1938, but this was widely condemned as unworkable and in fact was never implemented during its lifetime. This difficulty and the outbreak of war in 1939 prevented any further practical steps towards establishing the Way before 1945.

Nevertheless, despite the pressures of the war and of the years immediately after it, valuable preparatory work was done. First, by the Scott Committee of 1942 which, although concerned primarily with land use in rural areas, considered proposals for the creation of National Parks, access in wild country and the establishment of long distance footpaths, one of which was the Pennine Way; secondly, by the Dower Committee of 1943 which looked at the establishment of National Parks in England and Wales; and finally in 1947 by the Special Committee on Footpaths and Access to the Countryside, which met under the chairmanship of Sir Arthur Hobhouse. This last was concerned with the preservation and maintenance of public rights-of-way, the creation of new ones, access to the countryside generally and the provision of long distance and coastal paths. It strongly supported the creation of a Pennine Way and recommended procedures by which other long distance footpaths could be created.

In May 1949 the National Parks and Access to the Countryside Act was passed. This created a National Parks Commission (later renamed the Countryside Commission) and laid down a procedure (still adhered to) by which long distance routes could be created. Although this Act did not meet all the demands of walkers, it was nevertheless a measure of considerable importance.

Under the provisions of the Act the procedure was divided into three stages:

(1)   A report proposing the new route is prepared by the Commission and submitted to the appropriate Secretary of State. This report shows the proposed line of the route, a statement of which paths already exist and which new paths have to be created; and finally an estimate of the cost of creating and maintaining the route. The Commission is obliged by law to consult every Joint Planning Board, County Council and County District Council through which the way goes, although in recent years they have tended to consult more widely, with, for example, landowners and other interested organizations. If considerable opposition is found at the consultation stage, particularly from local authorities, then it is very unlikely that the Commission will proceed (as happened, for example, with the Cambrian Way) as it would then be very difficult, if not impossible, to complete the work needed for creation. The Pennine Way was the first long distance route to be considered by the Commission and the proposal for it was presented to the Minister for Local Government and Planning, Hugh Dalton, in June 1951.

(2)   The Secretary of State approves (or rejects) the proposals with or without modification. This is referred to as the designation. The Pennine Way proposals were approved without modification on 6 July 1951, that is, in exactly fifteen days (still the record for speed of approval).

(3)   The Secretary of State writes to each of the local authorities involved and asks them to begin work on the project. The Countryside Commission will at this stage agree a programme of work with the authorities and will provide in full the necessary finances. In the case of the Pennine Way this was a very lengthy step (as it has been with other routes): 61 miles (98 km) had been created by 1957, but it took a further eight years to create the remaining 9 miles (14 km). The policy of the Countryside Commission has been to proceed by agreement,

Pennine Way 'furniture' at Rapishaw Gap, Hadrian's Way (Day 16)

but local authorities may make Creation Orders if agreement cannot be reached. Virtually all creations for the Pennine Way were by agreement, and indeed few such Orders have been made for the long distance routes generally.

The Pennine Way was finally opened at an official ceremony on Malham Moor on 24 April 1965 (see page 162). (As the 1949 Act did not apply to Scotland the final section of the Way to Kirk Yetholm was not finally completed until 1977 under the authority of the Countryside (Scotland) Act 1967, although walkers had been finishing along it from the beginning. One consequence of this was that extra funding then became available for work on that section.)

Once a long distance route has been opened it must be maintained. The actual work is done directly or is contracted out by the local authorities through whose area the path runs. The Countryside Commission agrees a programme of work with each authority annually and then provides financial support for it (originally the cost was fully met by the Commission, but this subsidy has now been reduced to 75%).

From time to time official modifications to the route are proposed by the local authorities concerned. In the case of the Pennine Way there have been twenty-two suggested diversions to the route since it was first designated, of which the majority have been approved (the largest of these, in the vicinity of Cauldron Snout in Teesdale, involved about ½ mile/800 m of path). Most of these modifications were made before the route was officially opened and there have been few since then. It is likely that there will be further changes, but they will probably affect only a very small part of the route. The Countryside Commission advises walkers to follow waymarks even where this will take them away from the route described. Long distance routes established under the auspices of the Countryside Commission are now called National Trails.

One problem not foreseen at the beginning was that of erosion, particularly over areas of blanket peat at the southern end of the route. In an effort to combat this, the Pennine Way Management Project (jointly promoted by the Peak Park Joint Planning Board and the Countryside Commission) was launched in 1987. Its objective is to produce a long-term management framework for the southernmost 40 miles (64 km) of the Way and for a further 10 miles (16 km) in the Oldham/Rochdale area. The Management Officer will report on the lessons of the project when it ends in 1990.

Appropriately, the fiftieth anniversary of the article in the *Daily Herald* that began it all was celebrated by a gathering of several hundred walkers on Malham Moor on 22 June 1985. The principal guest was Tom Stephenson, at the age of ninety-two.

TOM STEPHENSON

Tom Stephenson was born in Chorley, Lancashire on 12 February 1893, the eldest of nine children. He spent his early years with his grandparents, but returned in 1900 to his parents at Whalley, a village about 6 miles (10 km) from Blackburn. (It was not uncommon in those days for older children in large families to stay with relatives or friends.) On leaving school at thirteen he started work as a labourer in a local calico printing works and worked there until he was twenty-two.

Whalley, on the northern fringe of the Lancashire industrial belt, is surrounded by beautiful country. Tom Stephenson's love of walking probably began with the ascent of Pendle Hill, near his home. This was followed by a walk to the Lake District, alone and sleeping out along the way. No mean achievement for a boy of fourteen! Around the same time, he developed a deep interest in the countryside—particularly in geology—and in writing, which brought him some limited success with local papers. Finally, out of this period came his life-long and deeply held socialist beliefs.

His interest in geology led to evening classes at Burnley, to which he cycled, and to a scholarship at the Royal College of Science (now one of the constituent colleges of Imperial College of Science, Technology and Medicine). His political views led to imprisonment as a conscientious objector during the First World War and to the cancellation of his Scholarship. After the War he returned to the textile industry, but left to work for the Labour Party, first as a local agent then at its national office.

The early 1930s mark the beginning of his deep involvement with the walking movement, although he had been an active walker for about twenty-five years by that time. In one way or another, this involvement was to last over fifty years. In 1933, on the strength of his early articles, he was offered the post of rambling and open-air correspondent with the *Daily Herald*. He accepted and stayed with the newspaper until World War II. It was in this period that he wrote his famous article on the Pennine Way.

Stephenson became secretary of the Ramblers' Association in 1948, a post he held for twenty-one years, although in an unpaid capacity until 1952. He was one of the founders of the Pennine Way Association and, with Edwin Royce, its first secretary. The Association surveyed the route and acted as a pressure body to get it established. He served on the Hobhouse Committee, which dealt with footpaths and access to the countryside generally and specifically with the creation of long distance footpaths, and later on the National Parks Commission. His friendship with leading figures both in the walking world and in the post-war Labour government, and his position as secretary of the Ramblers' Association, put him in a unique position to influence events at a time when important legislation was being enacted.

In many ways Tom Stephenson was ideally suited to his role at that particular time. Although he showed a respect for the views of others, he never hesitated to put forward his own opinion in a forthright manner. He was perhaps single-minded, but only in the sense of having interests that were obviously related and that he vigorously pursued, and not in a way that limited the breadth of those interests. To the end he remained a good orator—dogmatic, perhaps; but never bombastic—using 'key word' cards to keep him on the right lines. His integrity and the sincerity of his beliefs were never in question and many people who are activists today are so because of him.

Tom Stephenson retired as secretary of the Ramblers' Association in the autumn of 1968, and the occasion was marked by a dinner at the National Liberal Club the following February. The speakers were Barbara Castle MP, who had been a member of the early rambling parties up the proposed line of the Pennine Way; Lord Strang, Chairman of the National Parks Commission at the time of its official opening; and, of course, Stephenson himself.

He was President of the Association for three years after his retirement as secretary, continuing to take an active role in its affairs. His great retirement work, however, was a history of the access movement, *Forbidden Land,* which was published in 1989. His last mountain walk was taken in his early eighties, but he continued to ramble until he was over ninety. He died in Stoke Mandeville Hospital on 28 February 1987 at the age of ninety-four. In his will he left most of what he owned to the Ramblers' Association which was by far the largest bequest it has ever received.

Inevitably, the name of Tom Stephenson will be associated by most people primarily, even exclusively, with the creation of the Pennine Way. Certainly it was an event of great significance, but it should be viewed as only a part of a much wider—and a more important—struggle: the securing of walkers' rights generally. In that wider field no other person has yet played a more important part. When the unquestionable right of walkers to open access on mountain and moorland areas is finally conceded and the ways taken by walkers properly safeguarded, that success will be firmly rooted in his work.

Pennine Way waymark, Graining Water
(Day 4)

It was Tom Stephenson's wish that no monument should be erected to him, even along the Pennine Way. For that reason, suggestions to rename it the Stephenson Way or the Stephenson Trail should be ignored. The general health and vigour of the walkers' movement provides a far more satisfactory memorial—and one that would certainly have met with his approval.

An Outline of
the Way

Above: Wind sculptured millstone grit,
Kinder plateau (Day 1)

The Geology of the Pennines

Overall the Pennines are fairly simple in structure and relatively uniform in composition. The rocks from which they are formed originated almost entirely as deposits in sea, coastal or deltaic conditions in the Carboniferous period, 220 to 350 million years ago.

The first deposits were formed in warm, shallow, clear tropical seas—the British Isles were around the equator at that time—and consisted of the remains of the abundant—and now extinct—creatures and plants which inhabited them; these were later to form enormously thick beds of white, pure limestones (Great Scar Limestone). Later the clear seas were replaced by the delta of a great river and the deposits formed came from mudflats and sandbanks; these gave rise to soft shales and sandstones separated by bands of a less pure limestone. Even later, this river brought down large quantities of sharp, angular particles, produced by the erosion of a mountain range which lay to the north; this was to produce a thick layer of hard and durable millstone grit. Finally, the land surface rose sufficiently to allow dense forests to develop in coastal swamps; the remains of trees and other vegetation from these forests compacted later to produce coal.

It must be emphasized that conditions changed both with time and locality throughout the Pennines and the deposits formed would change correspondingly. The picture is not, therefore, completely uniform.

The end of the Carboniferous and the beginning of the Permian period, which followed it, were marked by great earth movements and the rocks which now form the Pennines were raised in a great anticline (an arch) running in a north-south direction. In the Peak District the fold was substantially symmetrical, but to the north there was a pronounced asymmetry, with a much steeper side to the west. The Pennines of the present day are the much-eroded residue of this anticline.

In a few places, older rocks, which lie under those of the Carboniferous period, emerge on the surface. Malham Tarn owes its existence to a small exposure of impermeable Silurian slates, formed nearly 100 million years earlier; a similar exposure can be found in Crummack Dale, where boulders of

dark Silurian rock stand on pillars of limestone left after erosion of the surrounding surface. These, however, are few in number and limited in area.

In the south of the Pennines, from Ashbourne to Castleton, the overlying shales and millstone grit of the anticline have now been stripped away, exposing the thick underlying layer of limestone. This limestone is seen again further to the north in the Craven district of Yorkshire. Northwards from Edale—and again north of Wensleydale—the shales and millstone grit are predominant, producing the harsh acidic moorlands so characteristic of the Pennines. The three peaks of Pen-y-ghent, Ingleborough and Whernside and, further north, Great Shunner Fell and Cross Fell, owe their shape to their caps of millstone grit. The Coal Measures are now entirely absent from the Pennines, but can be found on both flanks where the great coalfields are situated (some thin seams of coal do exist, however, below the millstone grit).

The Cheviot Hills, to the north of the Pennines, were formed in the Devonian period, which preceded the Carboniferous, and consist of igneous rocks formed by volcanic action. Initially there were violent eruptions which threw out great masses of debris, but these were soon followed by extensive lava flow producing layers thousands of feet thick. Much later, long after the products of these eruptions had cooled and solidified, a massive surge of molten rock (magma) took place deep within the earth. This in turn solidified to produce a hard granite, which can be seen nowadays in the area of The Cheviot where erosion of part of the overlying lava and agglomerate has left it exposed. These igneous rocks must have stood out from the seas of the Carboniferous, as a series of limestones, shales and sandstones (the Cementstone Group), almost surround them.

A similar phenomenon took place at the end of the Carboniferous when hot magma was forced up vertical fractures. These intrusions were later to form a hard, dark rock called dolerite whose resistance to erosion has produced some spectacular outcrops. The Whin Sill, used by Hadrian to great advantage in the building of his wall, the Farne Islands and the eminences on which the castles of Bamburgh and Dunstanburgh were built, are among them.

The Stainmore Gap (Day 10)

THE PHYSICAL GEOGRAPHY OF THE PENNINES

The Pennines are a range of hills about 145 miles (233 km) in length and varying between 20 miles and 40 miles in width (32–64 km), running in a north-north-easterly direction from the Stoke-on-Trent/Derby/Nottingham area in the south to the Tyne valley in the north. The range forms the main watershed of northern England and has been deeply cut by streams which flow into the Irish Sea to the west and the North Sea to the east.

It is not a mountainous area in the normal sense, for very little of the range lies over 2000 ft (610 m); it is better described as upland, most of which is between 1000 and 1500 ft in height (305–457 m). In the lowland areas on each side of the Pennines—and particularly in the south—large conurbations have grown up, based originally on the proximity of extensive coalfields. Because of these, ease of transport from one side of the Pennines to the other has been an important requirement. This was achieved reasonably easily where valleys cut through the hills, but such routes were always insufficient and had to be augmented by the construction of steep roads, which took a tortuous path to reduce the difficulties, or by the driving of long canal or railway tunnels through the ridges of high ground.

The Southern Pennines, which end at the Edale valley, are the remains of an eroded anticline so that limestone has been exposed over a wide area. The result is a limestone plateau about 1000 ft (305 m) in height with ridges of acid moorland down each side often edged with long, thin crags of millstone grit. Most of the forest which originally covered this plateau has long since been stripped away and the woodland there nowadays is mainly the result of deliberate planting. This is an area of 'improved' grassland, extensively used for dairy farming. In a few places the plateau has been deeply cut by rivers, such as the Dove and Manifold, which have become famous because of their beauty. Drainage, however, is good and there are numerous dry valleys and some rivers which flow only in the winter months, when rainfall is high.

The Central Pennines, which run from the Edale Valley to the Aire Gap, are a region of high millstone grit moors. The thin soil cover is very acidic and, combined with high rainfall and poor drainage, has produced an environment in which only a few plants, such as heather, bracken and cotton grass, can grow. The result is a bare, bleak, dark and boggy landscape; an endless vista of rolling, swelling moorland hills. The edges of the moors have been deeply cut by river valleys which are often dammed to supply local industrial towns in the lowland regions with water. Industry and towns crowd in on each flank and often

penetrate deeply where the valleys permit.

From the Aire Gap the Pennines continue for another 70 miles (113 km) to the Tyne valley. Usually referred to as the Northern Pennines, this region may be divided into two sections, the Askrigg and Alston Blocks, which are separated by the broad Stainmore Pass, the highest and least important of the three main natural trans-Pennine crossing points. Limestone has again been exposed over large areas of the Askrigg Block, but massive faulting and more vigorous ice flow during the Ice Age have produced a more dramatic landscape than that in the Southern Pennines. This area is characterized by great cliffs such as Malham Cove and Kilnsey Crag, limestone pavements and extensive cave and pot-hole systems. In the Alston block the Pennines reach their maximum height (2930 ft/893 m) in the Cross Fell and Mickle Fell massif. An enormous fault on the west side of Cross Fell has produced the great western face which drops down steeply into the Eden Valley in marked contrast to the gentle eastern slopes.

The Cheviot Hills lie to the north of the Tyne Gap in an arc about 45 miles (72 km) long inclined in a north-easterly direction. The main ridge consists of a series of tops about 1600 ft (500 m) high gradually rising to a maximum of 2674 ft (815 m) at The Cheviot. As with the Pennines, the ridge is a major watershed, mainly between the heads of east-flowing rivers.

A PROFILE OF THE WALK

From Edale the Pennine Way makes an easy start, following Grindsbrook Clough as it climbs up to the southern edge of the Kinder Scout plateau. As the clough steepens, the going becomes harder, but the real business of the day does not begin until the plateau itself is reached. Featureless and with numerous groughs and peat bogs, the plateau gives a tough walk, best crossed on a compass bearing until one of the tributaries of the River Kinder is reached. From there the sandy bed of the river gives easy walking until the edge is regained at the Kinder Downfall.

The far edge, with its tors of weathered gritstone, is followed for a short distance until a steep descent can be made to the moor below. The remainder of the way to the Snake Pass—crossed at its highest point—will be remembered mainly for its wetness and for the endless detours necessary to avoid patches of bog.

The Snake gives little respite, however, for the traverse of Bleaklow—which is equally tough—starts immediately. The Way climbs slowly to the isolated tor of Hern Stones, then across desolate peat bog to the summit at Bleaklow Head. From there the going becomes easier as the Way changes direction and heads westwards, following Torside Clough in a long descent into Longdendale.

Black Hill beyond Longdendale has a bad reputation among Pennine Way walkers, but this is based only on a short, hard section around the summit. The section beyond, over White and Black Mosses, was once far worse, but substantial work has now vanquished most of its terrors. Past Black Moss Reservoir the Way reaches Standedge, famous for its engineering works, although much of it lies out of sight underground.

North of Standedge the moors continue; their difficulties, however, are insignificant compared with those already encountered. A special bridge was constructed to take the Way over the M62, before the rise to Blackstone Edge. The Edge is composed of millstone grit crag and boulders from which superb views can be obtained.

From the Halifax-Littleborough road, several miles of easy walking—the first on the Way—take the walker by reservoirs and along low moorland edges towards the Calderdale valley, which is crossed at one of its narrowest points, thus avoiding the busy industrial towns nearby. As always on the Pennine Way, however, civilization is quickly left behind and once you are out of Calderdale the moors are soon reached again.

Near the Gorple reservoirs The Pack Horse Inn will refresh weary travellers as it did when the packhorse trains came that way carrying goods between local communities. At Walshaw Dean the Way enters Brontë country, passing buildings known to the sisters and used in their novels. Ickornshaw Moor is the last stretch of rough country before the Aire Gap and marks the end of the Central Pennines. For the next 18 miles (29 km) the Way passes through fields, along canal towpaths and streamside paths which give a welcome respite from moorland walking.

Malham lies at the southern edge of the limestone area of the Yorkshire Dales, and this geology is soon evident in the immense cliff of Malham Cove and at Great Close Scar above Malham Tarn. Fountains Fell is climbed by an old miners' track which served mine workings on its summit and another takes the Way down to the lonely farm of Dale Head, which once provided overnight fare for drovers and packmen. The fine mountain of Pen-y-ghent is traversed and the long descent from there to Horton in Ribblesdale passes pot-holes hollowed out by streams many thousands of years ago.

Walled lanes and green tracks used in centuries past by travellers, drove herds and packhorse trains take the walker over Cam Fell and across the slopes of Dodd Fell, high above the

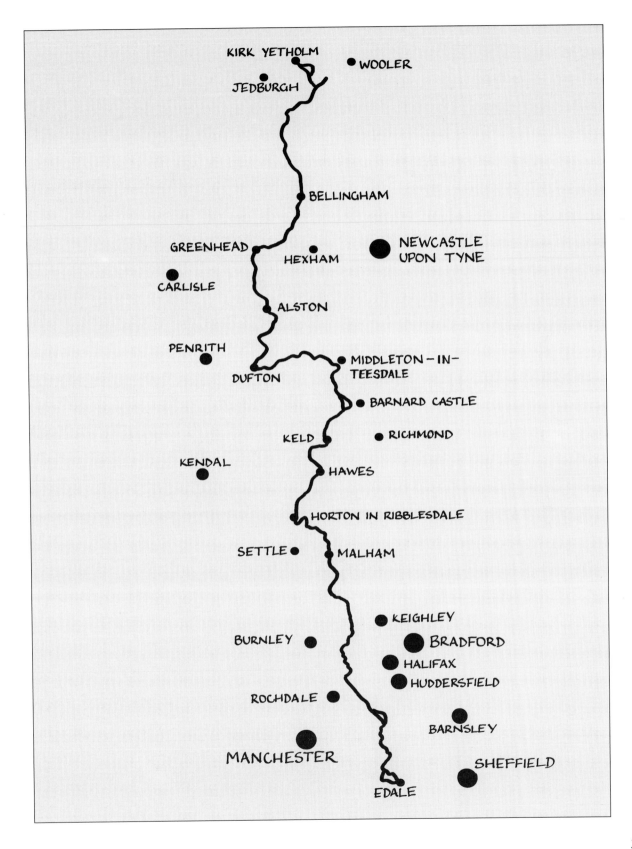

Signs used on maps

ROUTE	DIRECTION OF ROUTE
STREAM WITH BRIDGE	CRAG
ROAD	HILL OR MOUNTAIN TOP
RAILWAY	YOUTH HOSTEL
ENGLISH-SCOTTISH BORDER	BUILDINGS
HADRIAN'S WALL	EARTHWORK OR FORT
CONIFEROUS WOOD	DECIDUOUS WOOD
LAKE OR RESERVOIR	NORTH

SCALE OF LARGE ROUTE MAPS

0   1   2   3 MILES

0   1   2   3   4   5 KM

Note: The starting and finishing points for each day's walking are indicated by the number of the appropriate Landranger map followed by a six-figure grid reference. Thus, the starting point for Day 1 will be found at grid reference 123860 on Landranger sheet no. 110.

deep valley of Snaizeholme, to Hawes, a market town in Wensleydale. By the waterfall of Hardrow Force the Way starts a long climb to the summit of Great Shunner Fell, a magnificent view-point. The descent brings the walker to Swaledale, regarded by some as the finest of the Yorkshire dales and the original home of the Swaledale sheep which are now found throughout the Pennines.

From Keld the Way follows West Stones Dale to lonely Tan Hill Inn, the highest in England, and over Sleightholme Moor to God's Bridge and the busy A66. Baldersdale and then Lunedale are crossed before the Way reaches Middleton at the start of Teesdale. The walk along Teesdale is undoubtedly one of the most enjoyable parts of the Way. High Force—the largest waterfall in England—and the rapids of Cauldron Snout are the main attractions, but on a fine day almost every step of the way will be appreciated. Beyond the lonely farm of Birkdale the Way heads over moorland to rise eventually onto the rim of High Cup, a valley carved out by a glacier during the Ice Age. In the next valley the village of Dufton offers excellent hospitality.

The day out of Dufton is the longest and hardest of the Way. Four mountain tops have to be crossed, of which the last is Cross Fell, the highest summit of the Pennines. From Cross Fell the descent is made down an old way, along which corpses were once taken to the nearest consecrated ground, which leads by the workings of disused lead mines. By Garrigill, Alston and Slaggyford the Way continues north, following the valley of the South Tyne and the Old Maiden Way, along which supplies were fed to Hadrian's Wall. At its end the Way meets the Wall near Greenhead. This is the end of the Pennines, but the Way continues eastwards along the central—and best—section of the Wall where it runs along the Whin Sill.

Near the Roman fort of Housesteads the Way leaves the Wall and heads north again. The country between here and Byrness is generally low-lying, but very lonely and now much afforested. Most walkers will take two days over this section, stopping overnight at Bellingham.

The long, undulating ridge of the Cheviot Hills, along the border between England and Scotland, is a fitting finish to the Pennine Way. Just before the Roman Camp at Chew Green the Way joins the Border Fence and accompanies it over a series of minor tops. Only the more determined will continue to the end in one day and most will descend for a final night into one of the flanking valleys. A short diversion should be made to the summit of the Cheviot, but after the Schil, which comes soon after this, there are few problems and the Pennine Way finishes, as it began, on an easy note.

THE WALK

DAY 1

THE HIGH PEAK:
Edale to Crowden in Longdendale

STARTING POINT
Grindsbrook Booth, Edale (110-123860)
FINISHING POINT
Crowden in Longdendale (110-068991)
LENGTH
15 miles (24 km) [Alternative 1½ miles (2.5 km) further]
ASCENT
2150 ft (650 m) [Alternative has approx. 300 ft (90 m) more climbing]
TERRAIN
There are some easier stretches, eg. along the Kinder edge from the Downfall and following the course of the Kinder River, but mostly the route is over rough and boggy moorland. The most difficult sections are over the Kinder plateau and across the top of Bleaklow. An alternative route uses field paths then a farm road, before climbing to the plateau edge and following it to meet the main route at the Downfall. A tough introduction to the Way.
REFRESHMENTS
Cafés, shop and hotel/public houses in Edale; none on the route.
ACCOMMODATION
Youth Hostel, hotel/public houses and guest houses at Edale. Youth Hostel at Crowden.

'There is indeed an extended angle of this county . . .. which they call High Peak. This, perhaps, is the most desolate, wild, and abandoned country in all England . . . The tops of these hills seem to be as much above the clouds, as the clouds are above the ordinary range of hills.'

Daniel Defoe, *A Tour Through the Whole Island of Great Britain, 1724–1726*

Know as Aidele in Domesday Book and Eydale in 1305, the name Edale is probably Old English in origin and means 'the island valley'; a beautiful description, for the Vale of Edale is indeed an island, surrounded almost entirely by high and desolate moorlands. On that account it was for many centuries an isolated place relying for its trade and supplies on the packhorse trains which came into the valley. As late as the seventeenth century it lacked even a chapel, and both worshippers and the dead had to go over to nearby Castleton. The opening up of Edale began in the eighteenth century when a mill was built there which attracted workers from the Hope Valley, and developed when the railway came in 1894.

Nowadays, Edale is one of the busiest centres in the Peak District, with an Information Centre, two cafés, two inns, a camp-site, a Youth Hostel and a large car-park. It remains, nevertheless, essentially a walkers' village and there is no other in the whole of England that is more closely associated with the rambling movement. The Pennine Way could easily have been started further south so that the White Peak, which is very much a part of the Pennines, was included, but that would have broken Tom Stephenson's stipulation that the route should be a high-level one. Once the decision was taken to start the Way in

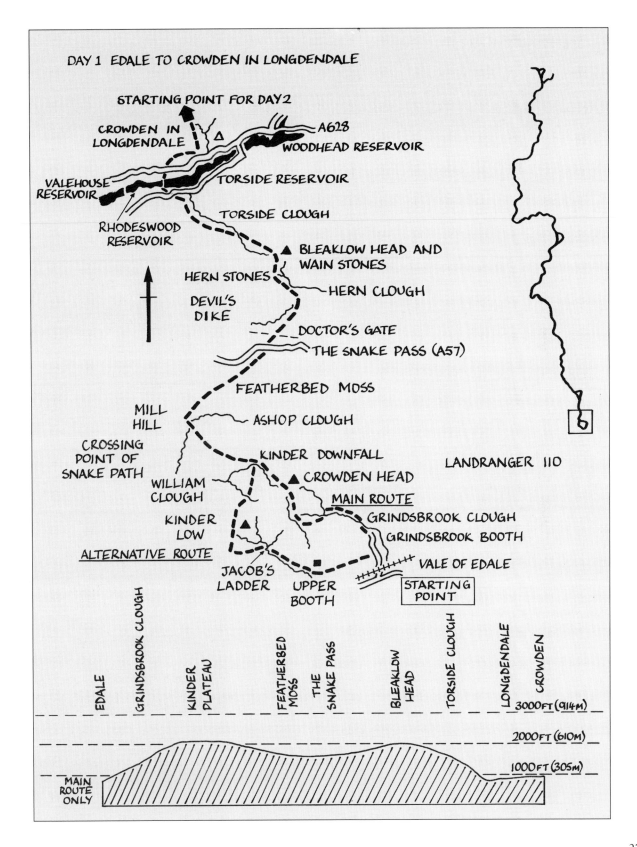

DAY 1 EDALE TO CROWDEN IN LONGDENDALE

STARTING POINT FOR DAY 2

CROWDEN IN
LONGDENDALE

A628

WOODHEAD RESERVOIR

VALEHOUSE
RESERVOIR

TORSIDE RESERVOIR

RHODESWOOD
RESERVOIR

TORSIDE CLOUGH

BLEAKLOW HEAD AND
WAIN STONES

HERN STONES

HERN CLOUGH

DEVIL'S
DIKE

DOCTOR'S GATE

THE SNAKE PASS (A57)

FEATHERBED MOSS

MILL
HILL

ASHOP CLOUGH

CROSSING
POINT OF
SNAKE PATH

KINDER DOWNFALL

LANDRANGER 110

CROWDEN HEAD

WILLIAM
CLOUGH

MAIN ROUTE

GRINDSBROOK CLOUGH

KINDER
LOW

GRINDSBROOK BOOTH

ALTERNATIVE ROUTE

VALE OF EDALE

JACOB'S
LADDER

UPPER
BOOTH

STARTING
POINT

EDALE

GRINDSBROOK CLOUGH

KINDER PLATEAU

FEATHERBED MOSS

THE SNAKE PASS

BLEAKLOW HEAD

TORSIDE CLOUGH

LONGDENDALE

CROWDEN

3000FT (914M)

2000FT (610M)

1000FT (305M)

MAIN
ROUTE
ONLY

27

the High Peak, Edale was the obvious choice.

Before leaving Edale a decision has to be taken on the route, for there are two choices as far as the Kinder Downfall. In essence, the main route, which goes up Grindsbrook Clough and crosses the Kinder Scout plateau, is shorter but rougher; the alternative, which goes along the Vale to Upper Booth and then approaches the Downfall more slowly over Kinder Low, is longer (by 1½ miles/2.5 km), and involves more climbing, but is more interesting. Both cross rough ground, the main route over open moor and the alternative along an edge, so that in bad weather there is little to choose between them. In the end the decision will probably depend upon the ability to navigate: those who are confident in it will probably choose the main route; those less so will perhaps think the alternative better, for the Kinder plateau is a very frightening place to be lost on. (A wall memorial in Edale church to three Rover Scouts who died on the Four Inns Walk in 1964 is a salutary reminder of how hostile local moors can be.)

There is little at Edale to indicate that the longest footpath in Britain starts there. A few small signs direct the walker up a lane by the Old Nag's Head and over the famous footbridge—made from a single tree trunk—which crosses Grinds Brook. Neither is there any indication in the first mile (1.6 km) or so of the difficulties that lie ahead, for the Way follows an easy and pleasant path through fields on a slow climb towards the Kinder plateau. Higher in the clough, however, the path steepens considerably and climbs over boulders until a final short scramble leads onto the plateau.

For those who have no experience of the High Peak the plateau is likely to come as a shock. But in fact the Way avoids some of its worst horrors by striking initially westwards across the outlying spur of Grindslow Knoll and then following the edge for a short distance before heading out across the plateau. The crossing is best done on a compass bearing until one of the tributary streams of the Kinder River—recognized by its sandy bed—is encountered. From then on, everything is straightforward and the walk along the river, which gradually grows wider, but not appreciably deeper, is extremely pleasant. In thick mist it is important to remember that the river flows eventually over a cliff at the Kinder Downfall and a change from sand to rocks should be regarded as a warning of its approach.

At the Downfall the Kinder River comes over the edge of the bed of millstone grit which caps the plateau. Although impressive at all times, the Downfall is undoubtedly at its finest

The start of the Way: the log footbridge over Grinds Brook.

THE GRITSTONE MOORS

North of Edale the predominant rocks of the Pennine moors are those of the Millstone Grit series, made up of hard, highly resistant gritstone and soft, black, easily eroded shales. The gritstone can be seen as occasional isolated tors and long 'edges', while the shales are most easily inspected on moorland flanks where streams have cut deeply into them. Although the gritstone contains some useful minerals, the rock is porous and soluble materials are quickly washed away. The result is a thin, poor, acidic soil cover in which few plants can survive.

Layers of peat up to 16 ft (5 m) thick cover the high plateau and gently sloping shoulders of moorland. It is thought that these began to form at the end of the Ice Age, about 8000 years ago, in the waterlogged and anaerobic conditions of blanket bogs. Such areas are characterized by the presence of an unbroken surface cover of bog mosses (sphagnum moss). Under these conditions little decay takes place, resulting in a gradual build-up of dead material. Erosion is characteristic of most peat areas, with the surface cut by deep channels (groughs) or into isolated mounds (peat hags).

At present, however, there are comparatively few areas where a continuous moss cover survives and consequently where new peat is still being formed. It is likely that the blame for this change must be laid—as usual—at man's door. The place of the moss has been taken in most cases by heather or by cotton sedge.

Heather covers very large areas in the Pennines, usually favouring those parts where the rainfall is lower, or pronounced slopes where the drainage is better. Left to themselves heather moors will support a wide variety of plants, but in practice this is rarely the case as most heather moors are regularly burnt to 'improve' them for grouse shooting.

In a few small areas such as gritstone edges or the upper margins of woodland belts, where the soil is dry and some shade may be obtained, bilberry can be found; rarely, however, in such profusion or with sufficient vigour to make the gathering of its dark, almost black, berries—which make pies of superlative flavour—worth the effort.

Finally, some patches of deciduous woodland—remnants of a great forest which once covered much of the moorland area—still linger on, usually on slopes where the roughness of the ground has given them some protection.

Eroded gritstone near the Kinder Downfall

in the depths of winter when the fall freezes into a magnificent cascade of ice, or on days of storm when the wind, gathering strength as it converges up the valley, flings the fall high into the air as a cloudy spray. In the summer, when the sun beats down and the stream is reduced to a mere trickle, the Downfall is an ideal place for a short siesta.

Instead of heading straight for the plateau, the alternative way takes a more circuitous route up the Vale of Edale, following the line of an old packhorse way which went over to Hayfield via Barber Booth. Barber Booth—like all other 'booths' in the valley—was originally a temporary shelter for cattle which later developed into a small settlement. Further along, the Way crosses a superb packhorse bridge at the bottom of Jacob's Ladder. The Ladder—thought to be named after Jacob Marshall, who cut steps up the steep slope—had become dreadfully eroded two or three years ago, but considerable repair work has now been done by the National Trust; perhaps not to everybody's taste, but it is much safer and pleasanter to climb than it was before. Shortly afterwards, the Way goes to the north, striking over Kinder Low and along the plateau edge to join the main route at the Downfall.

In contrast to the interior of the plateau, all the edges are firm and give superb walking, so little time will be taken over the mile (1.6 km) or so which follows the Downfall. Where the ridge tapers out the Way drops steeply down to the flat moor below and up to Mill Hill. On the rise to Mill Hill the Way crosses the Snake Path which runs from Hayfield to the Snake Road. This was the scene of the famous Mass Trespass of 24 April 1932 when several hundred ramblers were involved in a confrontation with gamekeepers and police. Over fifty years on the rights and wrongs of that day still provoke heated debate.

It is difficult to say much—and not a lot that is good—about the section from Mill Hill to the Snake Pass for the way is wet and lies over flat, featureless moorland. In clear conditions the main interest, after the first mile (1.6 km) or so, is likely to focus on the cars and lorries coming over the moor on the busy Snake Road, although your own arrival there is likely to seem somewhat delayed.

The present road over the Snake Pass was constructed by Thomas Telford as a turnpike in 1821. It was named, not after its circuitous course, but after the Snake Inn which is about 2½ miles (4 km) away on the Sheffield side. This, in turn, was named after the Duke of Devonshire whose crest was a snake and who was the owner of the inn and large areas of surrounding moorland. Earlier users of the pass included the Romans who in the first century AD built a road over it which

The Packhorse bridge below Jacob's Ladder on the alternative route

Right: The Kinder Downfall under
summer conditions

Below: The descent into Longdendale by
Torside Clough

ran from a fort near Brough to one near Glossop. It became known as Doctor's Gate from its association with Dr John Talbot, an illegitimate son of the Earl of Shrewsbury, who used to travel over it frequently during the fifty-five years that he was vicar of Glossop. Doctor's Gate runs roughly parallel with the road a few yards to the north.

Beyond Doctor's Gate the Way has been diverted into the bed of a long shallow groove, Devil's Dike, which gives excellent walking as it rises slowly up the moor. Where this ends, however, a bad section has to be crossed before Hern Clough is reached. From this point it is best to follow the clough, later choosing one of its tributaries which has a sandy bed and which heads in the right direction, rather than attempting to take a direct line to the Hern Stones. The only difficulty lies in choosing the point to make an exit, for the high banks of bare peat block all views.

There is little to become excited about on reaching the Hern Stones, although they provide much comfort to wanderers in these peaty wastes. Worse lies ahead, and the way to the next point of note, the Wain Stones near Bleaklow Head, is as rough as it comes. At the Wain Stones, however, although several miles of walking still lie ahead, the main difficulties of the day are now behind.

Going in a curve to the north-west the Way picks up the upper reaches of Torside Clough and follows it down into Longdendale on an airy path which runs along the edge of the moor high above the stream. Only the crossing of the dam of Torside Reservoir and a short walk through some rough fields is then necessary to complete the day.

There is no doubt that Longdendale—the valley of the river Etherow—has seen better days. There was perhaps even a time when it was a place of peace and beauty. But all that lies very much in the past and certainly before man got his hands on it. It is a perfect example of what can happen when he decides to exploit and use an area without caring too much about the likely result. Normally, it would be a place to be hurried through, with the night spent somewhere quieter and more congenial. Unfortunately, however, on the Pennine Way there is very little choice, for only bleak and hostile moors lie ahead until Standedge is reached, and that is much too far away for the average walker. The only consolations are a first-rate Youth Hostel and camp-site although both are near the busy A628.

DAY 2

BLACK HILL AND THE WESSENDEN ALTERNATIVE:
Crowden in Longdendale to Standedge

STARTING POINT
Crowden in Longdendale (110-068991)
FINISHING POINT
Standedge (110-021096)
LENGTH
9 miles (14 km) [Alternative 1½ miles (2.5 km) further]
ASCENT
1250 ft (380 m) [Alternative has approx. 650 ft (200 m) more climbing]
TERRAIN
A long climb following the course of Crowden Great Brook to the summit of Black Hill, followed by two stretches of fairly featureless moorland. The summit area of Black Hill can be difficult. The alternative via the Wessenden Reservoir has more scenic interest.
REFRESHMENTS
Public houses at Standedge.
ACCOMMODATION
Bunkhouse at Standedge and accommodation off-route in nearby towns.

'All Derbyshire is full of steep hills, and nothing but the peakes of hills as thick one by another is seen in most of the County which are very steepe which makes travelling tedious, and the miles long . . .'

Celia Fiennes, *Journeys,* 1697

At one time Crowden was a thriving village with shops, public houses, a school, a chapel and a fine house, Crowden Hall, which was built by the Hatfield family in 1692. Work for this community was provided by several quarries, a bleach works and a cotton mill, and later by the railway and the construction of the reservoirs. Crowden even enjoyed the benefits of having its own railway station from 1860 to 1957. The railway line which served this station ran between Manchester and Sheffield and was opened in 1845. Some distance to the east of Crowden it ran through the Woodhead Tunnel, about 3 miles (5 km) long, whose construction cost the lives of at least thirty-two navvies. The five reservoirs in the valley were built between 1848 and 1877 and together produced an almost continuous stretch of water nearly 6 miles (10 km) in length. With these developments completed, however, the community slowly disappeared and today Crowden is represented by little more than the Youth Hostel (originally a row of railway workers' cottages), a few houses and a camp-site.

From Longdendale the Pennine Way follows the left bank of Crowden Great Brook—a tributary of the Etherow—in a great

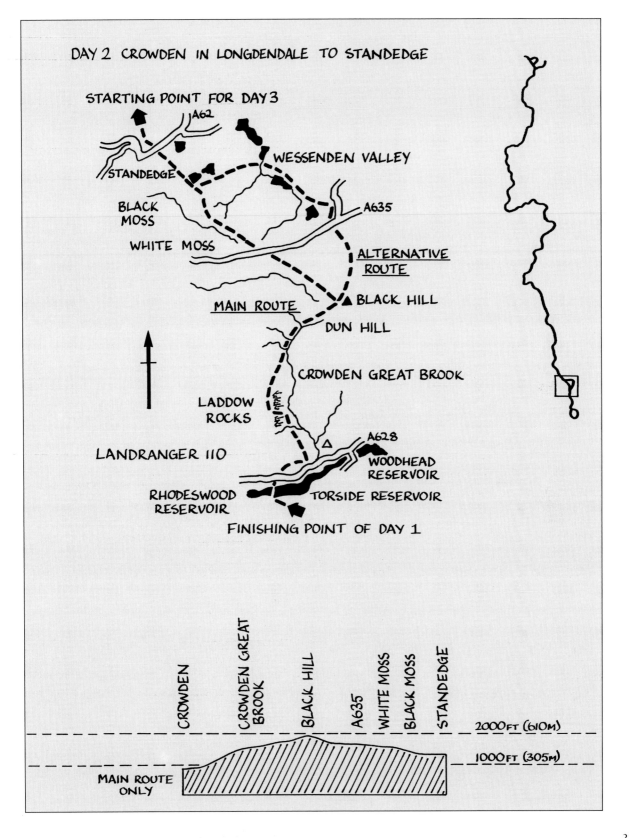

DAY 2 CROWDEN IN LONGDENDALE TO STANDEDGE

STARTING POINT FOR DAY 3

A62

WESSENDEN VALLEY

STANDEDGE

BLACK
MOSS

WHITE MOSS

A635

ALTERNATIVE
ROUTE

MAIN ROUTE

BLACK HILL

DUN HILL

CROWDEN GREAT BROOK

LADDOW
ROCKS

LANDRANGER 110

A628

WOODHEAD
RESERVOIR

TORSIDE RESERVOIR

RHODESWOOD
RESERVOIR

FINISHING POINT OF DAY 1

CROWDEN

CROWDEN GREAT
BROOK

BLACK HILL

A635

WHITE MOSS

BLACK MOSS

STANDEDGE

2000FT (610M)

1000FT (305M)

MAIN ROUTE
ONLY

curve to the north until Dun Hill, about ½ mile (800 m) short of Black Hill. A long, but comfortable, walk on which the miles and the climbing slip by almost unnoticed. There are two places where steep climbs have to be made, but both are short and of little account; the first is at Rakes Rocks where the hillside falls back into a great amphitheatre of gritstone crag and steep boulder slopes, and the second which takes the Way to the top of Laddow Rocks. It is easy to succumb to the temptation to avoid the second of these by taking an apparently easier line beneath the rocks, but this path should not be taken, for it is eroded and far inferior to the firm and airy path along the top.

Laddow Rocks is one of the main climbing faces in the Peak District and was one of the earliest crags to be opened up. Care is also needed where the path levels out along the top of the crag, for another—and initially much clearer—path leaves the edge to the left and there is a tendency for walkers to follow it. This path leads over Laddow Moss to Chew Reservoir in a different direction to the Pennine Way.

Black Hill has acquired a bad reputation among Pennine Way walkers. This is unfortunate, for the way from Crowden to the summit is mainly a fine walk, firm and acceptably dryish, until the summit area is reached. It is only here, in perhaps the last 200 yards (180 m) or so, where the walker has to cross bare peat and some rather slimy channels, that the difficulties of Black Hill are concentrated. Even so, except in very wet conditions, care and a willingness to make detours should ensure that even these problems are negotiated without too much trouble.

The actual summit of Black Hill is called 'Soldier's Lump' because it was used as a military survey point. Timbers from a theodolite-stand used in 1784—not by the Ordnance Survey which was not founded until seven years later—were discovered here in 1841 and are now in the Science Museum in London. The prominent mast to the south-east of the summit is at the Holme Moss Television Station and is 750 ft (230 m) high.

From the summit of Black Hill there is a choice of two ways. The main route goes more or less straight towards the north-west across Wessenden Head Moor to the A635, Oldham-Holmfirth road, which it crosses at the Greater Manchester-West Yorkshire boundary, before proceeding over the flatish expanse of White Moss. Beyond the immediate summit area the way is clear, following a line of cairns and posts, and no particular problems should be encountered until the road is reached. The alternative route goes roughly northwards to reach the A635 much further along at Wessenden Head near its

Climbers on Laddow Rocks

junction with the Meltham road. This junction was once the site of the romantically named Isle of Skye Inn, one of the inns reached in the Four Inns Walk held annually on the moors of the Dark Peak.

Only a few years ago the mere mention of the name White Moss would have been sufficient to bring a pallor to the face of even the most enthusiastic of Pennine Way walkers. In those days it was extremely boggy, the worst stretch of walking along the entire way. Fortunately, the worst terrors of the moss have now been tamed by the laying of a long length of artificial footpath made up of palings. (Those venturing off the palings will soon find that the moss is as boggy as ever!) Beyond the end of the prepared path the going is still rough, with some muddy eroded sections and one or two bad groughs, but it is all manageable by following a line of cairns and posts across the relatively featureless moor of Black Moss.

Even with these improvements, however, the alternative is probably the best route, for the Wessenden valley is a welcome haven after the inhospitable moors which have been crossed since Edale. Nevertheless, it does suffer the two disadvantages of being longer by about 1½ miles (2.5 km) and involving a climb to make up for the height lost on the descent into the valley.

The summit of Black Hill

Either way, the walker will eventually find himself on the dam at the corner of Black Moss Reservoir, from where is it only a short distance to the Oldham-Huddersfield road where it crosses the high ground of Standedge. Although the day has been fairly short, few walkers will think seriously of venturing further.

Wessenden Reservoir

DAY 3

BLACKSTONE EDGE:
Standedge to the Calder Valley

STARTING POINT
Standedge (110-021096)
FINISHING POINT
The Calder Valley between
Todmorden and Hebden Bridge (103-971265)
LENGTH
16 miles (26 km)
ASCENT
1050 ft (320 m)
TERRAIN
Long rolling stretches of moorland rising up to Blackstone Edge, followed by easy walking along reservoir roads. Final long descent to the Calder Valley.
REFRESHMENTS
Hotel/public houses on the A58 after Blackstone Edge, near Mankinholes and in Calder Valley.
ACCOMMODATION
Mankinholes Youth Hostel off-route about 3 miles (5 km) from the valley. Guest houses in Calder Valley.

'. . . then I came to Blackstone Edge noted all over England for a dismal high precipice and steep in the ascent and descent on either side . . .'

Celia Fiennes, *Journeys*, 1698

The Pennine Way reaches the Oldham-Huddersfield road at its highest point where it crosses Standedge at a height of 1270 ft (387 m). Dog-legs on each side are evidence of the difficulties that the road builders must have had in surmounting it. The real glory of Standedge—and its claim to fame as a trans-Pennine crossing-point—lies, however, not in the road itself, but in the canal and railway tunnels which cut through the ridge about 600 ft (180 m) below.

The canal tunnel, which accommodates the Huddersfield Narrow Canal, has a length of 3 miles 418 yards (5.2 km) and is the longest canal tunnel ever constructed in Britain. Cut by rough blasting, it took seventeen years to complete and was not opened until 1811, at a cost of £160,000. The canal, which had seventy-four locks, was the second of the three great waterways which crossed the main watershed of the Pennines; the others were the Rochdale (completed 1804) and the Leeds & Liverpool (completed 1816). It was closed in 1944—a black time for

The crossing of the M62

42

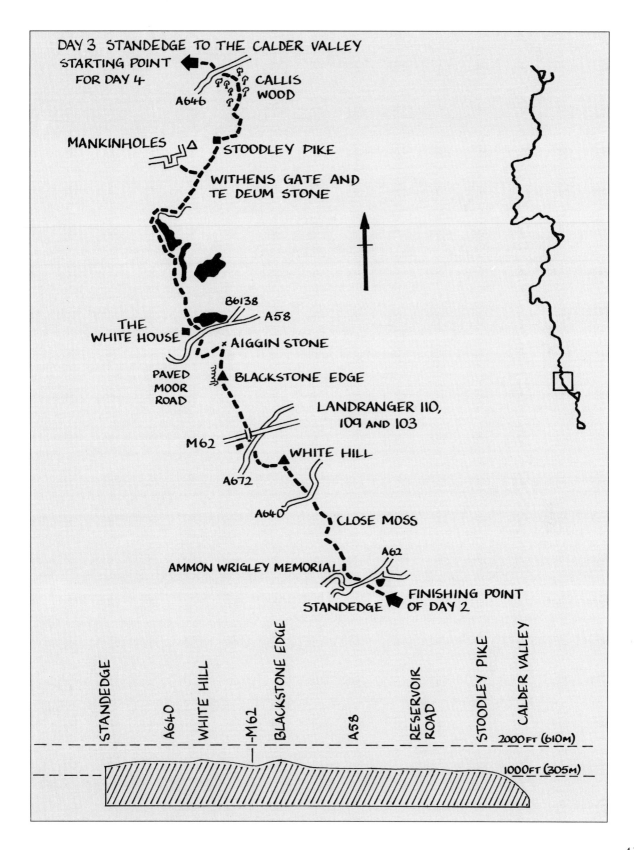

canals—although work is now under way to re-open parts of it. The tunnel is barred to casual visitors by massive gates at each end, but undergoes a regular inspection every other year.

The railway tunnel was constructed, parallel to the canal, by the London & North Western Railway in 1849 to provide a new route to Leeds from Liverpool and Manchester. As the company also owned the canal, cross-adits were cut so that waste material could be removed along it. The original tunnel—the longest railway tunnel in England—could accommodate only a single line, but a second single-line tunnel was added in 1871 and a double-line tunnel in 1894. Only the double-line tunnel is still in use, carrying Inter-City trains from Manchester to Leeds.

From the road the Pennine Way follows Standedge, the exposed millstone grit edge giving an exhilarating walk with extensive views to the west. By the Dinner Stone there is a plaque to Ammon Wrigley, writer of Saddleworth folklore, prose and poems, whose ashes were scattered here in 1946. Two of Wrigley's daughters shared his love of Saddleworth, for both insisted that their ashes should join those of their father.

After 1½ miles (2.5 km) the Way leaves the firm edge path for a rougher and much muddier path up Close Moss. Little can be said for the section from here to the crossing of the M62: the views are unremarkable and the walking without much interest, and it is with some relief that the motorway is finally reached.

To Pennine Way walkers the crossing of any busy trans-Pennine road is always unwelcome. An intrusion into the solitude that they came here to find; an unpleasant reminder of the workaday world left behind, however temporarily. Of all the roads crossed on the Way the M62, with its continuous streams of noisy traffic, is undoubtedly the least welcome. Mercifully, the intrusion is brief.

The bridge over the motorway was built specially for the Pennine Way in 1970, the alternatives being a dash across the carriageways, which would undoubtedly have reduced severely the number signing in at Kirk Yetholm Youth Hostel, or an annoying detour along the A672, which cuts under the motorway a short distance away.

Beyond the motorway the Way heads up the moor towards Blackstone Edge, There have been great changes here in the past fifteen years or so. Virtually pathless in 1970, it is now eroded and there are several sections where repairs have been necessary. Near the top, however, the way improves and a profusion of cairns leads to the Ordnance Survey obelisk on the Edge. The obelisk is set on the top of a gritstone outcrop, a

The old road over Blackstone Edge

The Calder Valley

superb view-point over Littleborough and Rochdale.

The official line of the Way follows the edge northwards to the Aiggin Stone (an old guidestone) at the end of the edge and then straight on over Blackstone Edge Moor to The White House inn on the Littleborough-Ripponden road. However, few Pennine wayfarers cross the moor directly, preferring instead to go down the remarkable moor road on the Littleborough side. This moor road has a surface made up of rough stones set together with edgings and a grooved paving down the centre. It is given on Ordnance Survey maps as of Roman origin and has even been described by some authorities as the finest stretch of extant Roman road in Britain.

There is doubt, however, as to whether this paving ever felt the tramp of Roman feet. An alternative theory—and probably more plausible—maintains that it is a turnpike that was constructed, in part along the line of an old packhorse trail, about 1735. In any event it was superseded by another turnpike—the 'Old Road'— which was built about 1765. The present road follows the route of still another turnpike—the 'New Road'—built towards the end of the century. All these earlier ways can still be traced as footpaths or bridleways. The White House inn was originally called the Coach and Horses Inn and is situated where the Old and New Roads meet.

Northwards from The White House the Way follows a reservoir road—broad, even-surfaced and absolutely level—which has been described quite correctly as the easiest section on the Pennine Way. The reservoirs passed—Blackstone Edge, White Holme, Light Hazzles and Warland——were all constucted to maintain the level of the Rochdale Canal, which goes through the valley to the west, but are now used to supply water to local towns. The stretch is interesting for students of reservoir architecture, but everybody else will probably remember it best for making up the time lost in The White House, which was reached about lunch time.

Soon after the top reservoir the Way reaches an edge overlooking Calderdale—the green fields and buildings of the valley are the first sight of 'real civilization' since Edale, now well behind. At Withens Gate, recognized by a paved crossing path, a short diversion can be made to see the Te Deum stone. This is a rectangular monolith which gets its name from the inscription TE DEUM LAUDAMUS (We praise thee O Lord) cut into one face. The paving marks the line of an old packhorse trail which ran from Sowerby Bridge to the Calder Valley, and the stone was placed beside it to remind passing packmen that a

Old Ways in the Pennines: The Packhorse Trails

For about 500 years up to the early-eighteenth century the packhorse was the main—and usually the only—means of transporting goods. The main reason was the appalling state of the roads, which made the use of wheeled transport often difficult and at times impossible. An attempt had certainly been made to recify this situation: the Highways Act of 1555 had made each parish responsible for the repair of its own roads, but this initiative was largely a failure.

The development of turnpikes in the eighteenth century changed the situation. Turnpike Trusts, established by Act of Parliament, took over responsibility for the maintenance of sections of road; in return they recouped their costs and made a profit by levying tolls on all road users. As roads gradually improved and the use of wheeled vehicles increased, the packhorse began to disappear.

A packhorse train collecting lime from a kiln

The breeds most favoured were Galloway and German Jaeger. Up to fifty horses would form a train, each tied to those is front and behind. It was common for harnesses to be fitted with bells to warn other trains of their approach, for trails were very narrow. Each horse was fitted with a saddle on which rested two panniers, a load being about 2½ cwts (130 kg).

The loads varied considerably. Fish was taken from Workington to London, cloth from the Lancashire textile factories to Midland towns, lead from mines and Dent marble to the east coast ports for shipment to London. One important commodity was salt, taken from pits at Northwich and Middlewich to towns such as Sheffield.

The packhorse trains have now gone, but many signs of the trails that they followed can still be found, particularly in hill areas where the plough has not been at work on them. Holloways are common, sometimes following a single line up a hillside, sometimes with several parallel courses produced in turn as the original line became too eroded, or on steeper slopes taking a zigzag line to ease the severity of ascent and descent. Packhorse bridges—narrow, high-arched, with low parapets —can be found on many streams, often with holloways converging to them. Finally, there is the evidence of place-names: Kinder Scout has a Jaggers Clough on its eastern slopes, there is a Salter's Brook Bridge in Longdendale and on the Pennine Way near Hebden Bridge a Pack Horse Inn still provides refreshments for weary travellers.

Packhorse bridge at Wycoller

prayer would no doubt be good insurance. The way was also a corpse road along which coffins were taken to the nearest consecrated ground at Heptonstall and it was traditional for coffins to be laid by the stone for a short time.

Withens Gate is the point at which the Pennine Way is left by walkers intending to spend the night at Mankinholes Youth Hostel. Those heading for the Calder Valley continue along the edge to the prominent obelisk—Stoodley Pike Monument—which is at the far end.

It is likely that some sort of structure has stood on the Pike for many centuries. Local legends claim that this was a large cairn which housed the bones of a dead chief, while a map of 1795 indicates some kind of round tower topped with a cone. What is known for certain is that a monument, financed by local subscription, was built on the hill to commemorate the end of the Napoleonic Wars. As building was still in progress when Napoleon escaped from Elba, it was thought prudent to suspend operations and building was not resumed until after Waterloo. The tower suffered badly from neglect and finally fell down in 1854 (as this coincided with the declaration of war against Russia it gave rise to a local saying that the monument falls down when some national calamity is imminent!). The local inhabitants rebuilt it—although to a different design and prudently further back from the edge—two years later. Pennine Way walkers intent on getting their money's worth—and who have the energy—can carefully feel their way (part of it in pitch darkness) up the spiral staircase to the balcony for a glorious view.

Even at the end of a long day, which began at Standedge, the final stretch into the Calder Valley will be enjoyed, particularly the final stage through Callis Wood. Walkers who spent the night at Mankinholes must, of course, climb out of the valley and traverse the Pike at the start of a new day.

Stile near Stoodley Pike

49

DAY 4

BRONTË COUNTRY:
The Calder Valley to Ponden

STARTING POINT
The Calder Valley between
Todmorden and Hebden Bridge (103-
971265)
FINISHING POINT
Ponden Reservoir near Haworth
(103-995371)
LENGTH
12 miles (19 km)
ASCENT
1750 ft (530 m)
TERRAIN
Steep rise out of the Calder Valley,
then pastures, easy moorland and
reservoir road; final descent to
Ponden.
REFRESHMENTS
Hotel/public house at Widdop (at
about the half-way point) and
Ponden.
ACCOMMODATION
Hotel/public house and guest houses
in the vicinity of Ponden; also
Haworth Youth Hostel 3½ miles (5.5
km) away.

'. . . Our hills only confess the coming of summer by growing green with young ferns and moss in secret little hollows. Their bloom is reserved for Autumn, then they burn with a kind of dark glow, different doubtless from the blush of garden blossoms.'

Charlotte Brontë, 1851

The Pennine Way crosses the Calder Valley between Todmorden and Hebden Bridge. Here the valley—never wide at any point—narrows into a steep-sided, deep and well-wooded gorge, formed at the end of the great Ice Age of the Pleistocene period when the River Calder, swollen by immense quantities of meltwater, cut its way down through the layers of shale and millstone grit. (The name Calder is a compound of the Welsh *caled* and the Old British *dubro* and means 'violent water'.) Where hard-wearing rocks were encountered steep sections were produced, but where softer shales were met much more erosion took place and shelves were formed.

The earliest settlements in the valley were formed on these shelves—and particularly on the north side where they would enjoy longer periods of sun—instead of on the valley floor which was marshy and thickly wooded. Although clearance and drainage of the valley bottom took place from the fourteenth century, there were no major settlements there until the great developments in transport about four hundred years later. The turnpike of 1760, the Rochdale Canal of 1804 and the Manchester & Leeds Railway line of 1841, provided the means by which raw materials were brought in and manufactures taken out. Factories became established along their length, resulting in a shift of the population from the hillsides to the valley floor and the consequent decay of the shelf settlements. The factories and houses which fill the valley today, taking up all available space on its steep sides, are a product of the industrial revolution in the seventeenth and eighteenth centuries; the small hamlets,

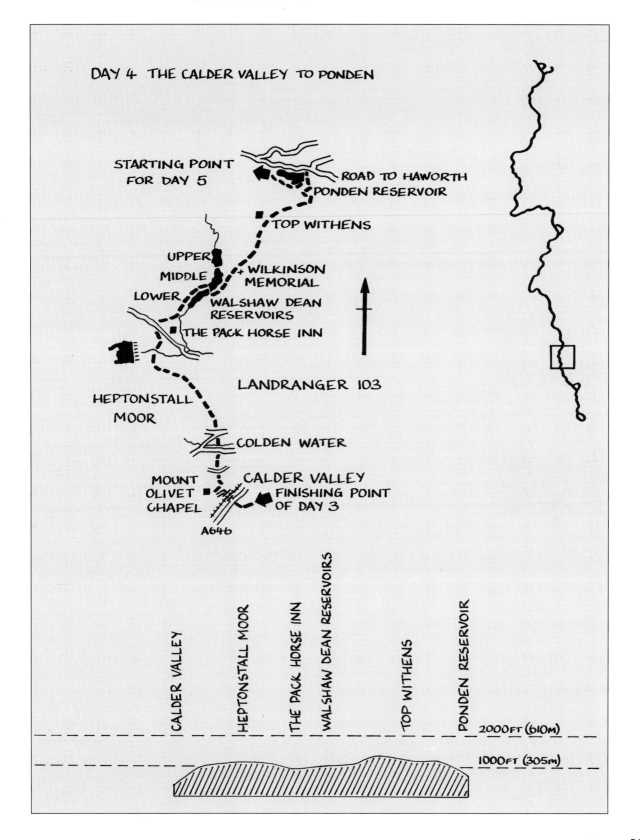

DAY 4 THE CALDER VALLEY TO PONDEN

STARTING POINT
FOR DAY 5

ROAD TO HAWORTH
PONDEN RESERVOIR

TOP WITHENS

UPPER
MIDDLE
LOWER

+ WILKINSON
MEMORIAL

WALSHAW DEAN
RESERVOIRS

THE PACK HORSE INN

LANDRANGER 103

HEPTONSTALL
MOOR

COLDEN WATER

MOUNT
OLIVET
CHAPEL

CALDER VALLEY
FINISHING POINT
OF DAY 3

A646

CALDER VALLEY

HEPTONSTALL MOOR

THE PACK HORSE INN

WALSHAW DEAN RESERVOIRS

TOP WITHENS

PONDEN RESERVOIR

2000FT (610M)

1000FT (305M)

such as Mankinholes and Heptonstall, are the products of an earlier age.

A walker crossing the Calder Valley by means of the Pennine Way has, therefore, to negotiate a series of steep steps broken by intermediate slopes of gentler gradient; the well-farmed northern hillside, with its numerous farmsteads and hamlets, standing in sharp contrast to the relatively barren and lonely southern slopes below Stoodley Pike.

Soon after you start the steep ascent from the valley, where the Way bends back sharply on itself, there is a small graveyard which belonged originally to Mount Olivet Chapel. The chapel ceased to be used long ago and was demolished, but the graveyard is still there; overgrown and neglected, surrounded by tall trees which give it some protection from the harsh weather of the Pennines. A place well worth a pause of a few minutes before the journey is resumed, for the inscriptions on the tombstones have a tale to tell of what life was really like in these parts a century or so ago.

On its rise out of the valley the Pennine Way moves far enough to the east to clip the end of Colden Clough, necessitating a descent and then an ascent on the far side. Hebble Hole Bridge, which crosses the Colden, is a lovely old bridge of large gritstone slabs, arranged in pairs. The Calderdale Way, a long distance footpath 50 miles (80 km) long which goes around Calderdale, crosses the Pennine Way at this bridge in its run along the northern slopes of the valley.

The moor top is reached shortly after a small housing estate which seems slightly out of place in this spot. After the long ascent from the Calder Valley the crossing of Heptonstall Moor will seem very easy and tame. In clear weather the main interest is likely to centre on the view to right over Hebden Dale, a noted beauty spot now owned by the National Trust, and the small isolated white building half-right, the Pack Horse Inn. The inn is on the road from Hebden Bridge to Nelson, which is reached soon after passing the Gorple Lower Dam Reservoir.

Old packhorse trails cross the moors in all directions in this area. One came from Burnley via Worsthorne and Widdop into the top of the Hebden Valley, another came up the valley and on to Colne, while a third came from Colne over Heptonstall Moor to Halifax, probably taking the line now used by the Pennine Way. The Pack Horse Inn, which was built about 1610, would have been a meeting point and over-night stop for the packmen who travelled on all those trails. Forty years ago it was virtually unchanged, and even today after some modernization it retains

Footbridge, Graining Water, Heptonstall Moor

THE BRONTË SISTERS

Haworth and the Brontë sistes—Charlotte, Emily and Anne—are so closely associated that it is often forgotten that they were not born there but at Thornton, near Bradford, where their father, Patrick Brontë was the incumbent. Patrick had married late in life a Cornish woman, Maria Branwell. Their six children were born over the next seven years, the youngest of whom was only three months old when the family moved the few miles to Haworth Parsonage.

The year following their arrival Mrs Brontë died of cancer; the effect on the children immediately and in the long term was traumatic. A warm and affectionate father might have done much to lessen the harm; but Patrick Brontë was not of that sort. Even their first experience of school—three years later as boarders at Cowan Bridge—only added to their distress: discipline was harsh and conditions bad, and the two eldest girls died of diseases contracted there. The three remaining daughters and their brother, Branwell, drew in on themselves, creating imaginary worlds which they wrote about in tiny notebooks.

Their first published work was a joint effort (excluding Branwell): a small collection of poems published pseudonymously at their expense in 1846. It was not a success, selling only two copies. Despite this, each sister began a full-length novel. Charlotte's *The Professor* failed to find a publisher (it was rejected nine times and eventually published posthumously), but her second, *Jane Eyre*, was accepted. It was published in October 1847 and was immediately successful and widely acclaimed. Emily's *Wuthering Heights* appeared two months later but received considerable criticism; its greatness was not recognized until long after her death. Anne's *Agnes Grey* was also published that year and was well received.

Tragedy, however, never seems to have been far away from the Brontë family. Branwell—addicted to both alcohol and drugs—died in September 1848 and Emily of consumption three months later. Anne died the following spring, shortly after the publication of her second novel, *The Tenant of Wildfell Hall*. Charlotte had two further novels published (*Shirley* and *Villette*) and became a literary celebrity. She was the only daughter to marry. Her marriage to her father's curate, Rev. Nicholls, was happy but tragically short: she died in 1855 after catching a chill while walking on the local moors.

The Parsonage at Haworth, the home of Brontë family

Above: A welcome sight for Pennine wayfarers: The Pack Horse Inn at Widdop

Opposite: Top Withens

much of its old character. Although slightly off-route, since it comes around midday, it is an exceptionally hard walker—or teetotaller—who passes it by.

A short distance beyond the inn the Way forsakes the open moor for a while and goes up a reservoir road into the valley of Walshaw Dean. There are three reservoirs in the Dean: the

Lower, Middle and Upper. The Pennine Way goes initially up the west side, later crossing to the east over the dam of the Middle Reservoir. On the banking of the reservoir, between the water and an overflow channel, rhododendrons have become established and are busily colonizing. First introduced into this country in the mid-seventeenth century, the shrub has become a menace in some areas and a lot of time and money is spent in controlling it. Beyond the reservoir the Way climbs the moor up a reconstructed path towards the north-east; on the rise there is a small memorial stone to 'E. Wilkinson. A Rambler. Died August 1964. Aged 35'.

As the top of the moor is reached the ruin of an old farmhouse comes into view. Known as Top Withens, it has long been associated with Wuthering Heights, the Earnshaw home in Emily Brontë's novel. As a result it is a place of pilgrimage for thousands of visitors each year. It was certainly there in the middle of the nineteenth century and must have been well known to the sisters, who lived only about 3 miles (5 km) away, but it could have had no resemblance to the building described by Emily Brontë. It is more likely that she used as her model High Sunderland Hall near Halifax, although she may have had the setting of Top Withens in mind.

The identification of places known to the Brontës and used in their novels is a popular pastime. Ponden Hall, a short distance further along, is thought to be Thrushcross Grange, the home of the Lintons, and Wycoller Hall, a few miles to the west, may have been the Ferndean Manor of *Jane Eyre*. But, whatever the merits of these associations, it is the moors themselves that really carry the spirit of the Brontës and there it is as strong as ever. Charlotte Brontë, after the death of her sisters, found the moors unbearable: 'My sister Emily had a particular love for them, and there is not a knoll of heather, not a branch of fern, not a young bilberry leaf, not a fluttering lark or linnet, but reminds me of her. The distant prospects were Anne's delight, and when I look round she is in the blue tints, the pale mists, the waves and shadows of the horizon. In the hill country silence their poetry comes by lines and stanzas into my mind; once I loved it; now I dare not read it.'

The long descent into the Worth Valley is a pleasant walk. A double-paved strip soon leads to a broad moorland track which passes between banks of heather. The farms of Upper and Lower Heights are passed—typical Pennine buildings of stone with flag roofs and small windows, the former built in 1761—before the final descent to the dam corner of Ponden Reservoir. Ponden Hall is to the left, the road to Haworth directly ahead over the dam.

DAY 5

INTO THE AIRE GAP:
Ponden to Thornton-in-Craven

STARTING POINT
Ponden Reservoir near Haworth
(103-995371)
FINISHING POINT
Thornton-in-Craven (103-908486)
LENGTH
12 miles (19 km)
ASCENT
1850 ft (560 m)
TERRAIN
Moorland (some rough), then field
paths.
REFRESHMENTS
Hotel/public houses at Ickornshaw
and Lothersdale.
ACCOMMODATION
Guest houses at Thornton-in-Craven;
Earby Youth Hostel 1½ miles (2.5
km) off-route and similar distance
from the end.

'Believe me, I've heard Guytrash rushing down the winter
winds.'

Halliwell Sutcliffe, *Through Sorrow's Gates*

From the end of Ponden Reservoir dam the Way follows a
rough farm cart-track which reaches the Laneshaw Bridge-
Haworth road at the far end of the reservoir where the infant
River Worth feeds into it. Ponden was one of three
reservoirs—the other two are Watersheddles and Lower
Laithe—built by the Borough of Keighley in the Worth valley;
Ponden and Watersheddles in the 1870s and Lower Laithe
about fifty years later.

There are few buildings at Ponden, but one is a gem. This is
Ponden Hall—one of the best-known guest houses on the
Way—passed a few minutes after leaving the dam. The present
building is a magnificent structure, both inside and out, whose
history is outlined on a stone tablet—now slightly difficult to
read—over the front door:

THE
Old houfe
now Standing was
built by Robert Heaton
for his son Michael,
Anno Domini 1634.
The old Porch and Peat
houfe was built by his
Grandfon Robert
Heaton A.D. 1680.
The prefent Building
was Rebuilt by his
defcendant R.H. 1801.

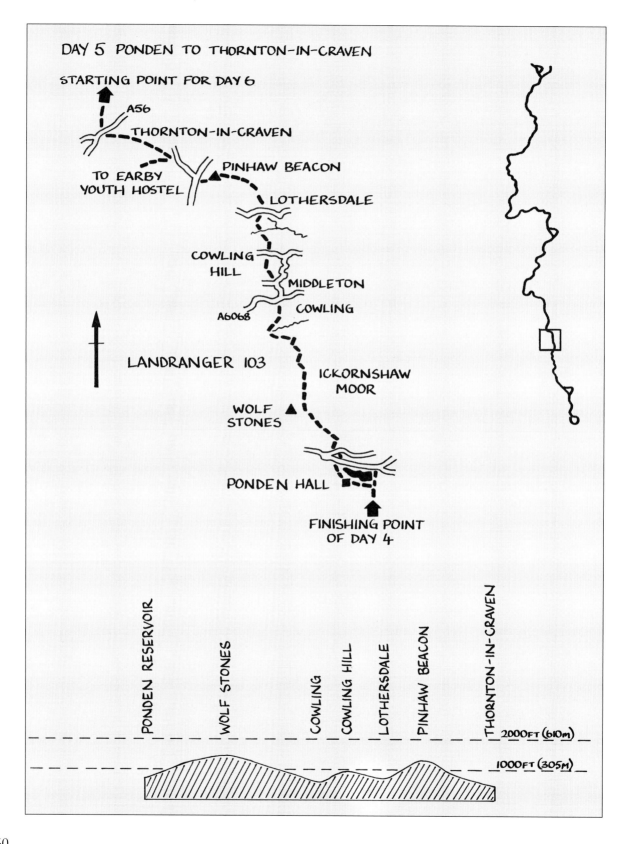

DAY 5 PONDEN TO THORNTON-IN-CRAVEN

STARTING POINT FOR DAY 6

A56

THORNTON-IN-CRAVEN

TO EARBY
YOUTH HOSTEL

PINHAW BEACON

LOTHERSDALE

COWLING
HILL

MIDDLETON

A6068

COWLING

LANDRANGER 103

ICKORNSHAW
MOOR

WOLF
STONES

PONDEN HALL

FINISHING POINT
OF DAY 4

PONDEN RESERVOIR

WOLF STONES

COWLING

COWLING HILL

LOTHERSDALE

PINHAW BEACON

THORNTON-IN-CRAVEN

2000FT (610M)

1000FT (305M)

DRYSTONE WALLS

Drystone walls are an important feature of the Pennines which will be seen almost every day of the Way from Edale to Kirk Yetholm. They are called drystone walls because they were built entirely from stone, using only mechanical bonding. This method of construction was not born of necessity as mortar had been available long before the walls were built; it was from choice because the builders knew through long experience that this produced a stronger and more durable structure. The long lines of walling which still stride across the Pennine uplands, two centuries or more after they were built, are a testimony to the soundness of that judgment.

Building drystone walls is an ancient art. It was used in the construction of Neolithic tombs some 4000 years ago and on the walls of Iron Age hillforts. The first drystone walls forming field boundaries were probably built around farmsteads and small villages to give pastures for grazing or to provide protection for the cultivation of crops.

Stile in drystone wall near Ponden Reservoir

Such enclosure was very limited, however, and by the end of the Middle Ages most of the land in England was still unenclosed: large, open fields were cultivated communally on a strip system by villagers who also shared grazing and other rights over areas of common land. This picture was to change drastically, although it took over 400 years, from the fifteenth to the nineteenth centuries, to accomplish it.

Early enclosure was limited and spasmodic—and often illegal. Nevertheless, by 1700 about half of the arable fields of England had been enclosed, although the overall pattern would be patchy. Much of Cumbria and Northumberland was enclosed, while other areas were hardly affected.

After 1750, however, the pace of enclosure quickened considerably. This was accomplished, not by the local actions of landowners, but by privately sponsored Enclosure Acts. The busiest periods were 1760–1770 and 1793–1815, during which some 3000 Acts were passed, the former period mainly concerned with open fields and commons, the latter with areas of waste land. The long, straight, sturdy walls of the Pennine uplands were the products of this legislation.

Although some enclosures were made after this period—the last important Act was for Skipwith in Yorkshire in 1903—the landscape seen today by the walker along the Pennine Way is substantially that which was established by about 1820.

Walkers who spend their night in the Ponden valley should note that this is the country of the Guytrash, a fiendish hound with huge eyes which haunts quiet country lanes. The mere sight of it is said to herald disaster. With another 210 miles (338 km) still left, it is as well to take no chances!

A short, stiff climb up lovely grassy paths leads to the higher Laneshaw Bridge-Oakworth road where it takes a dog-leg around a small side clough of the Worth. This road is the start of a long climb of 1½ miles (2.5 km) which ends near the Wolf Stones—a meeting point of three counties (Lancashire, West and North Yorkshire)—at about 1450 ft (440 m). For about half that distance the Way follows the line of a tall, sturdy and well-built wall, obviously a product of the Enclosure Period. Straight as a die the wall climbs, only to end abruptly on the open moor still some way short of the summit ridge. Work was obviously intended to go forward, for the cap stones have still to be placed on the final few feet and footings have been laid for several yards more.

The descent of Ickornshaw Moor is a rough bit of walking—reminiscent of parts of the Dark Peak—coming just when you thought that the worst was behind you! There is, however, a clear path over it, although you can see only a few yards at a time because of the roughness of the ground. The two monuments which can be seen half-right are Wainman's Pinnacle and Lund's Tower, two follies situated on Earl Crag, a thin gritstone edge which faces northwards over the Aire Gap. Peat is still cut on these moors—an uncommon practice nowadays—and drying stacks can be seen on its lower reaches.

One of the easiest sections of the Way—the crossing of the Aire Gap—starts at Cowling on the Colne-Keighley road which marks the end of the long descent from the Wolf Stones. From now on for about 18 miles (29 km) it is largely green fields, pleasant woods, grassy river banks and gentle hills. A lovely pastoral area given over to dairy farming rather than to mutton and wool. For the first time since leaving Edale, cows—mainly Friesians and Northern Dairy Shorthorns—will replace sheep as your main companions.

Cowling is made up of two hamlets, Ickornshaw and Middleton. The second, which is little more than two rows of small, terraced cottages, is passed on leaving the village. The first cottage on the left—indicated by a small plaque—was the birthplace of Philip Snowden. Although the son of a weaver—and therefore in the normal course of events destined to work 'in 't' mill'—he became a student-teacher at a local

The Aire Gap

Pinhaw Beacon

school and later entered the Civil Service as an exciseman. In 1927, however, he became converted to socialism and started a political career which led him to the House of Commons as MP for Blackburn and later as Chancellor of the Exchequer on three occasions. In his day he was formidable, both as an orator—said to be second in Labour circles only to Keir Hardie himself—and as a parliamentary debater. After his death in 1937 his ashes were scattered on Ickornshaw Moor. It cannot be a coincidence that those two rows of thirty or forty houses produced no fewer than three Labour Members of Parliament.

Two miles (3 km) beyond Middleton the Way reaches Lothersdale, a favourite stopping place for Pennine Way travellers. A single street makes up this village, which has much charm. Its name is derived from the Old English *loddere* and means 'the vagabond's valley'. Pinhaw Beacon on Elslack Moor beyond Lothersdale is the last major hill before the descent to Thornton-in-Craven. This is a superb view-point, particularly over the Aire Valley, crossed the following day. Walkers intending to spend the night at the Katherine Bruce Glasier

Memorial Hostel at Earby leave the Way shortly afterwards.

Katherine Glasier, one of the first graduates of Newnham College, Cambridge, became well known as a novelist and writer of short stories. With her husband, John Glasier, she devoted her life to social works. She lived from 1922 to 1950 in the hostel building (Glen Cottage)—named after her son, a man of exceptional promise, who died at an early age.

Others intent on reaching Thornton-in-Craven before nightfall continue on, slowly descending the moor. The disused railway line crossed just before the village was the Leeds & Bradford Extension Railway from Colne to Skipton, which was opened on 2 October 1848. The station at Thornton-in-Craven was a useful linking point for Pennine Way travellers for a few years until the line closed for passengers in 1970. A Roman road from Ribchester (Bremetennacum) to Ilkley (Olicana) ran through the village and there was a Roman fort nearby at Elslack. Today it is a pleasant place, with old stocks set on a small green, although perhaps unfortunate to be astride the busy A56, which carries traffic between Skipton and the Lancashire towns further south.

Thornton-in-Craven

APPROACHING THE DALES:

Thornton-in-Craven to Malham

STARTING POINT
Thornton-in-Craven (A56) (103-
908486)
FINISHING POINT
Malham (98-901629)
LENGTH
11 miles (18 km)
ASCENT
700 ft (210 m)
TERRAIN
Easy pleasant fields and riverside
paths.
REFRESHMENTS
Hotel/public houses at East Marton,
Gargrave, Kirkby Malham and
Malham; also cafés and shops at
Gargrave and Malham.
ACCOMMODATION
Youth Hostel, hotel/public house and
guest houses at Malham.

Clapper bridge, Langber Beck

'Ingleborough, Pendle hill and Pen-y-ghent,
Are the highest hills between Scotland and Trent.'

Old saying

Although the Aire Gap divides the Pennines into two nearly
equal parts, it is very far from being the half-way point of the
Pennine Way, which starts some distance up the Pennines and
finishes beyond them. It marks, however, a very definite stage
along the Way, between the bleak and barren gritstone moors of
the south and the limestone uplands of the Yorkshire Dales. By
the time he or she reaches Thornton-in-Craven, after five days
of heavy going over high and squelchy peat moors, the Pennine
Way walker has earned a change, an easy day and an early finish.
The crossing of the Aire Gap should provide all of these. But
make the most of it: Day 7, with two mountains to be crossed, is
not an easy one!

The lowland region beyond Thornton-in-Craven which is
traversed by the Pennine Way is drumlin country. Similar areas
occur elsewhere along the Pennines: in the Vale of Eden and at
Ribblehead north of Horton in Ribblesdale. Drumlins are still
somewhat mysterious things. It is clear that they were formed
during the last period of the Pleistocene Ice Age when sheets of
ice flowed down from the north-west over the area of the
Yorkshire Dales and into the Aire Gap. When these retreated
they left behind a thick covering of boulder clay (a mixture of
pebbles and boulders in a clay matrix). Usually this was laid as a
fairly even layer, but in a few places where the deposit was
particularly heavy it was formed into low hills, oval in shape
with their long axes parallel to the ice flow, and averaging about
150 ft (45 m) in height and ⅓ mile (500 m) in length. Exactly
how this came about is still not fully explained. From Thornton-
in-Craven to Gargrave the Way crosses a series of drumlins,

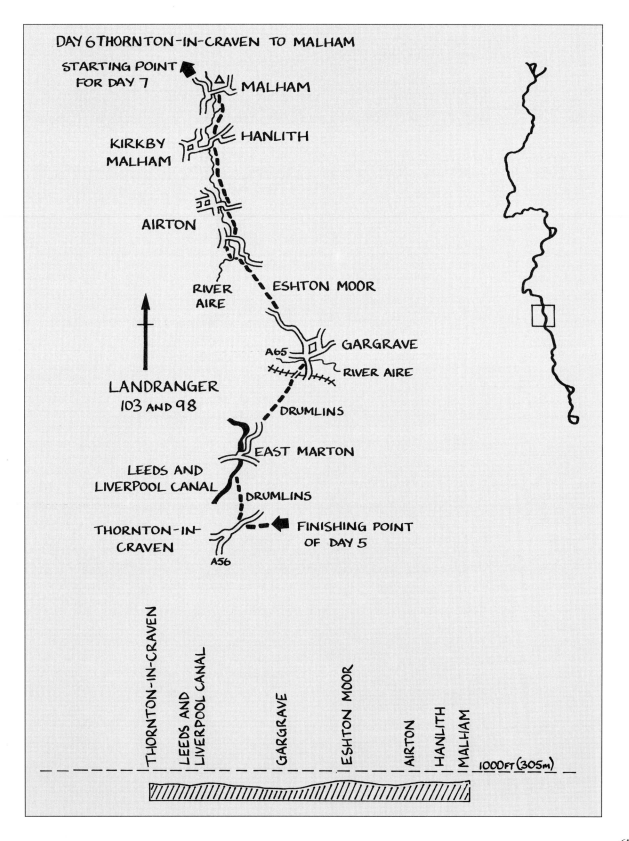

except for the middle section where it follows the towpath of the Leeds and Liverpool Canal for a short distance. The walk over the lovely green drumlins of the Aire Gap will be remembered for a long time.

The Leeds and Liverpool Canal is the last—and the most important—of the trans-Pennine waterways which are crossed by the Way. Although authorized in 1770, a through link between Leeds and Liverpool was not achieved until 1816, by which time both the Rochdale Canal and the Huddersfield Narrow Canal had been open for some years. The final product was 127 miles (204 km) in length with no fewer than ninety-one locks, including the famous Bingley Five Rise. Some great feats of canal construction were achieved on the Leeds and Liverpool. A total of twenty-three locks had to be built at Wigan; at Foulridge there is a 'Mile Tunnel' (actually 1640 yards/1.5 km long) where boats had to be 'legged through' before the arrival of a steam tug; and at Burnley the canal is carried over the town on an enormous embankment which was rightly considered as one of the Seven Wonders of the Waterways. Although it suffered from competition with the railways, the Leeds and Liverpool was affected less than most canals, probably because of the unusual size of its locks, which permitted exceptionally heavy loads to be carried on broad-beamed barges. Today it is the only one of the three to remain open, although only to pleasure craft.

The Way follows the canal towpath for nearly a mile (1.6 km) before another area of drumlins, longer than the first and even more delightful, takes the walker into Gargrave.

Gargrave was named Geregraue in Domesday Book and was not known by its present name until the twelfth century. It is a town of some substance, the first to be entered on the Pennine Way. A good place to take stock of supplies, for the next major centre is Hawes, two days hence. At Gargrave the Aire is met for the first time. The name Aire is probably derived from the Old Celtic word *isara* which means 'strong river', but at Gargrave it is a lazy river meandering along and forming loops and ox-bows across a narrow flood plain. On summer weekends Gargrave is a place to be avoided, for streams of cars flood through on their way to the Lake District or the Dales.

The first meeting with the Aire is brief, however, for beyond Gargrave the river swings in a great loop to the west and the Way cuts across over Eshton Moor to rejoin it south of Airton. The moor top between Harrows Hill and Haw Crag is a superb all-round view-point. The prominent whale-backed hill to the

The Leeds and Liverpool Canal near East Marton

south-west is Pendle, whose presence dominates the towns on the northern fringe of the Lancashire industrial belt. The area around Pendle is famous for its witches, a tradition that is still very much alive. Old Mother Chattox, Demdike and Alice Nutter are familiar characters to all who live in those parts. In a sense it was there that the Pennine Way began, for this was the hill that Tom Stephenson climbed as a boy in 1906 and that fired his love for walking. Alfred Wainwright was also inspired by it when he lived nearby at Blackburn, and the author, who was born in Nelson under the very shadow of Pendle, can testify to its charisma. It is no exaggeration to say that whole generations of Lancashire folk became walkers because they spent their formative years within sight of Pendle.

The Way rejoins the Aire just south of Newfield Bridge and then stays with it to its source at Malham. Even here, only 5 miles (8 km) from its source, the river is already some 30 ft (9 m) wide; a beautifully clean river gliding quietly between grassy banks or gurgling pleasantly over pebbly beds; glorying in a freshness that is to be all too soon destroyed.

Between Newfield Bridge and Malham the Way passes through two lovely dales villages, Airton and Hanlith, and near to a third, Kirkby Malham. Airton gets its name from the river for it means 'homestead near the river Aire'. Originally a Quaker stronghold, it has a small Meeting House, built in 1700, and a cottage in the middle of its triangular village green which was a squatter's house erected in the seventeenth century when land was scarce. Up the hill to the east is Calton Hall, the home of 'Honest' John Lambert who fought with Cromwell at Marston Moor and later died as a prisoner in Guernsey. Kirkby Malham is slightly off-route—and therefore better left to Day 7 if a rest day is taken at Malham—as the Way leaves the river and goes up an exceptionally steep hill through Hanlith (the name of the village was originally—and appropriately—derived from 'Hagena's Slope'). Near the bottom of the hill is Hanlith Hall, which has fine stone carvings.

The most exciting sight of the day, however, is kept for last: the great cliff of Malham Cove, seen for the first time from the hillside just beyond Hanlith. Limestone country lies ahead!

The River Aire at Hanlith

DAY 7

LIMESTONE COUNTRY:
Malham to Horton in Ribblesdale

STARTING POINT
Malham (98-901629)
FINISHING POINT
Horton in Ribblesdale (98-810721)
LENGTH
15 miles (24 km)
ASCENT
2600 ft (790 m)
TERRAIN
An interesting and fairly easy start by Malham Cove and Tarn; later the going gets tougher with ascents of Fountains Fell and Pen-y-ghent.
REFRESHMENTS
None along the way. Café and hotel/public house at Horton in Ribblesdale.
ACCOMMODATION
The nearest Youth Hostel is at Stainforth about 4 miles (6.5 km) from the end. Hotel/public house, bunkhouse and guest houses at Horton in Ribblesdale.

'JOHN DOWER 1900–1947 Architect and Town Planner, devoted his life to the cause of National Parks and preservation of the English countryside. He designed and built this hostel which was dedicated to his memory in 1948.'

Memorial tablet, Malham Youth Hostel

Walkers who started out from Edale nearly a week ago and who have been looking after themselves should by now be fit and running into a smooth routine of walking. If they are, then they should enjoy this day, which will take them from Malham to Horton in Ribblesdale through the Craven district of the Yorkshire Dales National Park. For superb walking, magnificent scenery and continuous interest this is the best single day's walking along the entire Way. Pray for a fine day here: partly because two mountains, Fountains Fell and Pen-y-ghent, have to be crossed, and partly because of the spectacular views.

The Way leaves Malham along the Langcliffe-Settle road following Malham Beck, which runs through the village. Three of Malham's four clapper bridges are passed along the way, the last of which is called Moon or Wash-Dub Bridge after Prior Moone, the last Prior of Bolton Abbey, who had it erected early in the sixteenth century. In monastic times, from about the twelfth century up to the Dissolution, the village was divided between two great religious houses with the stream as the boundary line: Fountains Abbey owned the manor of Malham West and Bolton Abbey that of Malham East.

At the end of the village the Way leaves the road and follows a footpath, still keeping with the stream, heading directly towards a great cliff, Malham Cove. The name Malham probably derives from the Old Norse for 'stony or gravelly place', a testimony to the difficulties that old settlers must have had in extracting a living from the soil. There are many signs of their

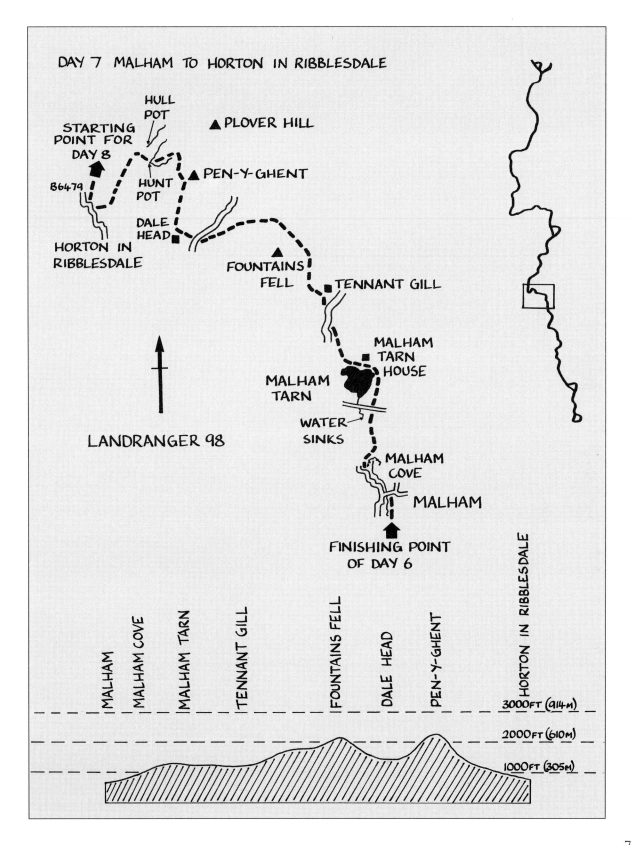

DAY 7 MALHAM TO HORTON IN RIBBLESDALE

HULL POT

PLOVER HILL

STARTING POINT FOR DAY 8

B6479

HUNT POT

PEN-Y-GHENT

DALE HEAD

HORTON IN RIBBLESDALE

FOUNTAINS FELL

TENNANT GILL

MALHAM TARN HOUSE

MALHAM TARN

WATER SINKS

LANDRANGER 98

MALHAM COVE

MALHAM

FINISHING POINT OF DAY 6

MALHAM

MALHAM COVE

MALHAM TARN

TENNANT GILL

FOUNTAINS FELL

DALE HEAD

PEN-Y-GHENT

HORTON IN RIBBLESDALE

3000FT (914M)

2000FT (610M)

1000FT (305M)

work along this stretch. Running down the hillside to the left of the path are Iron Age field boundaries and on the opposite side of the valley are a number of prominent broad terraces (called lynchets) which were cut from the hillside by Anglican farmers in the eighth century to provide a level strip which could be ploughed.

Malham Cove is immense, 240 ft (73 m) high and 900 ft (274 m) wide. Formed from Great Scar Limestone, it owes its existence to a massive fault, the Middle Craven Fault, which also formed the steep hillsides on each flank. The fault line now runs about ¼ mile (400 m) to the south of the Cove, which was eroded back to its present position by a torrent of glacial meltwater coming down from the moor behind. The waterfall which this produced at the Cove must have been an impressive sight. Sadly, the stream sank into fissures in its limestone bed long ago and now flows underground to re-emerge at Aire Head Springs just south of Malham. Records show that a waterfall was still there in the sixteenth century and even in the eighteenth it was able 'on occasions' to produce a magnificent cascade, but no water seems to have flowed over the lip of the Cove during the past 150 years or so.

It is said that hawks used to nest on Malham Cove's sheer—and in places overhanging—walls, but they have also gone, their place now taken by housemartins which wheel about the great face during the summer. Much rock climbing is done on the Cove, for this crag is considered by most climbers as the best in the dales, giving, as it does, very hard and exposed routes which are 200 ft (60 m) in length and it also has a magnificent traverse of 575 ft (175 m).

Such things are not for Pennine Way walkers, however, who out-flank the Cove by a path which rises steeply around the left-hand edge. Across the top is a superb area of limestone pavement, the finest stretch met with on the Way. The deep grykes give shelter for numerous plants, such as hart's tongue, wood sorrel and aspleniums, which thrive in moist, shaded conditions. At about the mid-point of the Cove a dry valley comes into the face to form the far perimeter of the pavement area. The official route continues up the hillside directly ahead and then crosses and slowly climbs the slopes to the east of the dry valley on a lovely grassy path. This is an old way called Trougate, once used by monastery traffic coming out of Malhamdale. Many walkers, however, turn up the dry valley until an escape can be made around a dry waterfall, Comb Scar. Both routes eventually reach the road south of Malham Tarn and then cross an area of rough pasture to the gate at the entrance of Malham Tarn Nature Reserve.

Malham Cove

LIMESTONE

The Pennines are formed almost entirely from sedimentary rocks laid down in the Carboniferous period, 220–350 million years ago. The first rock formed at that time was limestone, which now lies in a thick and substantially horizontal layer, several hundred feet thick, over a large area of the northern Pennines. Nowhere is this seen to better advantage than in the south-west of the Yorkshire Dales, where the limestone has been revealed by the removal of overlaying rocks and massive faulting.

Limestone, which is largely calcium carbonate, is a hard and durable rock—hence its widespread use as a road material —and, like most rocks, insoluble in pure water. But rain water, having absorbed carbon dioxide from the air to form a weak acid solution, can attack it and take it into solution. Evaporation of this solution will cause the carbonate to deposit as a solid. The two processes of solution and deposition over a long period are those responsible for the characteristic features of limestone areas.

One such feature is the comparative lack of small streams. Those that come into the area will usually flow for only a short distance before they disappear into the ground (at a sink), to reappear some miles away at a lower level. Dry valleys are often left below the sink which contain old stream beds, waterfalls and gorges. Others are 'summer dry' rivers which disappear in the warmer months, only to reappear in winter when the sink can no longer cope with the increased flow.

As water will usually take the easier line offered by the numerous vertical cracks and horizontal bedding planes that occur in limestone beds, these will be widened by chemical attack so that vertical shafts and cave systems may eventually form. Gaping Gill on Ingleborough has a shaft 20 ft (6 m) wide and 340 ft (104 m) deep, with known passages 9½ miles (15 km) long. Water seeping through joints in cave roofs produces stalactites, and stalagmites on the floor beneath. On the moor surface funnel-shaped depressions called shake holes are very common. These are produced by the gradual removal of the supporting limestone, causing the overlaying soil to subside over the years.

In a few places the upper surface of the limestone bed has been uncovered, such areas being referred to as pavements. Here water action has opened up the joints into wide crevices which have divided the flat surface into isolated blocks.

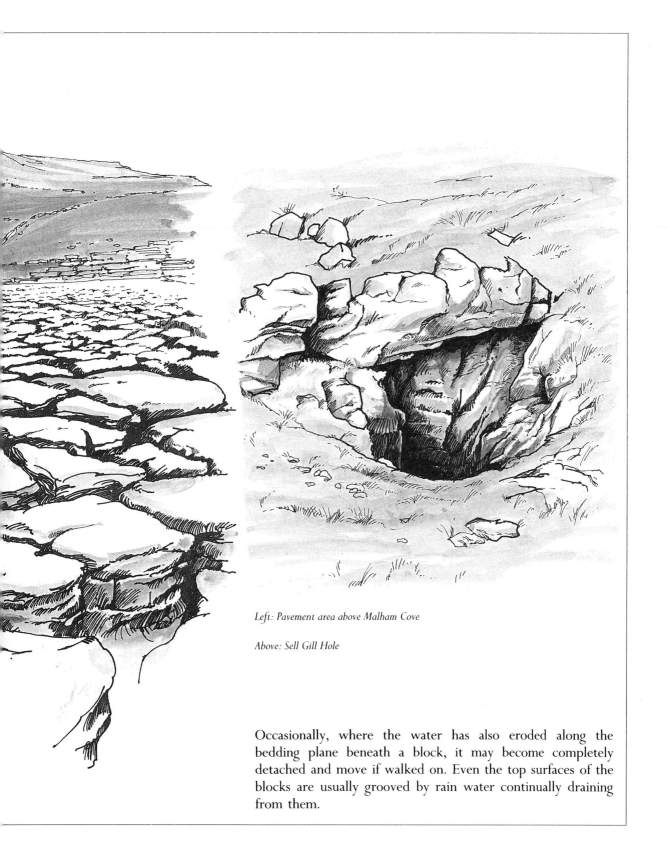

Left: Pavement area above Malham Cove

Above: Sell Gill Hole

Occasionally, where the water has also eroded along the bedding plane beneath a block, it may become completely detached and move if walked on. Even the top surfaces of the blocks are usually grooved by rain water continually draining from them.

This area was used in April 1965 for the official opening ceremony of the Pennine Way and in 1985 for the celebrations to mark the fiftieth anniversary of that famous newspaper article by Tom Stephenson. Much earlier it was an important crossing point of several old ways.

Malham Tarn, now directly ahead, is the highest lime-rich lake of any size in Britain and is of international importance for nature conservation. It owes its existence in a limestone area to another fault line, the North Craven Fault, which lies just to the south of the tarn, and the subsequent erosion of the hillside to expose older impermeable rocks beneath. It owes its present size to an embankment which was constructed in 1791 by Lord Lister, who owned the estate at that time. Little of the woodlands around the tarn is natural, most of it planted early in the nineteenth century.

The Pennine Way follows the estate road of Malham Tarn House, which runs around the eastern and northern shores of the tarn. The House was originally built as a shooting lodge by the same Lord Lister in the 1780s, but was extensively rebuilt in its present style last century by a late owner, Walter Morrison. It is now owned by the National Trust, which has let it to the Field Studies Council. Over 1500 students attend courses there each year.

At the north-west corner of the Reserve the Way leaves the estate road and goes northwards up a shallow dry valley. After about a mile (1.6 km), at Tennant Gill Farm the character of the Way changes abruptly as the long climb up Fountains Fell begins. This is one stretch which can, in all honesty, be said to lack interest. From the farm to the summit wall is about 2½ miles (4 km). Even on the best of days the climb up the bare moorland fellside will seem very long; on a day of mist and rain it will probably seem endless. To make matters worse, even the consolation of a mountain summit is missing, for the Way avoids it by about ¼ mile (400 m). (Purists will make the detour.)

Incredible as it may sound, the track up Fountains Fell, which the Pennine Way follows, was made in the late-eighteenth century to reach mine workings on the summit. Seams of medium-to-good-quality coal can be found just below the thin layer of millstone grit which forms the summit cap. Extraction of this by the sinking of bell-pit shafts began towards the end of the eighteenth century, the better coal going to smelt mills and for domestic use, the poorer being used for lime burning by local farmers or in commercial kilns at Settle and Malham. Production ceased about 1880. Two shafts—now fenced

The dry valley above Malham Cove

off—can be seen near to the path as the summit wall is approached.

If the ascent was long and monotonous, then the descent makes up for it. The way—down another old mine path—is shorter and crosses the northern face of the fell. The outstanding feature of the descent, however, is the superb view directly ahead of Pen-y-ghent, widely acknowledged—with the possible exception of Ingleborough—to be the shapeliest mountain in the Pennines.

The small farm of Dale Head at the end of the descent was a meeting place for drovers and packmen, for several packhorse trails and drove roads met here. Near here is the site of Ulfkill Cross, which was a boundary stone between the lands of Fountains Fell and Salley Abbey. The Pennine Way goes up the farm road past the farm and then up towards the southern ridge of Pen-y-ghent.

The summit wall of the mountain comes down the long south ridge and the Way keeps close by it, except at its mid-point where it is forced away by two crags and a boulder slope which cut across it. On a fine day the summit is a magnificent view-point—an ideal place to rest for a while, secure in the knowledge that all climbing is now behind and that only a long descent on a good path has to be completed before the day's finish at Horton.

Two pot-holes lie a short distance from the line of descent. Hunt Pot, which is nearest, is a sinister slit. Formed on a small fault at the upper limit of the Great Scar Limestone, it was first explored in May 1898 and contains three vertical pitches. Hull Pot, by contrast, has a huge opening 185 ft (56 m) long by 45 ft (14 m) wide, with a waterfall about half-way up its eastern side. Although the floor is normally dry, it can become covered with water during wet spells and there are even stories of the entire pot filling after exceptionally bad weather. The waters from both pots eventually find their way to the surface again at Brant's Gill Head near Horton, as does all the water from the western slopes of Pen-y-ghent and Fountains Fell.

The final stage is down a walled lane which finishes at the centre of Horton in Ribblesdale. The door of Pen-y-ghent café, which always gives a warm welcome to walkers, is only a few yards to the right.

Malham Tarn

DAY 8

THE CAM HIGH ROAD:
Horton in Ribblesdale to Hawes

STARTING POINT
Horton in Ribblesdale (98-810721)
FINISHING POINT
Hawes (98-873898)
LENGTH
14 miles (23 km)
ASCENT
1300 ft (400 m)
TERRAIN
Lovely green roads with gentle gradients along the line of old drove ways and the Roman road from Bainbridge into Ribblesdale.
REFRESHMENTS
None along the way. Numerous hotel/public houses and cafés in Hawes.
ACCOMMODATION
A Youth Hostel, hotel/public houses and guest houses at Hawes.

'Went from Askrigg to Ingleton 20 miles. . . . You then ascend for 5 miles incessantly and go on the top Ridge of a very high hill, called Cam, for about 5 more. As far as you can see, Black Moors are the only objects which present themselves to the Eye. This Road is so much exposed that by reason of the Snow it is often impassable for many days together, & the inhabitants of Askrigg and Ingleton talk of 'over Cam' as if it were in a different country.'

William Wilberforce, *Journey to the Lake District from Cambridge 1779*

Green roads—so called because they are not metalled—can be found throughout the Pennines—and for that matter in other areas—but those in the Yorkshire Dales always seem to have a special quality about them. Almost certainly they are of ancient origin, used down the centuries by Roman legions, monastic employees, packhorse trains, drove herds and travellers, as well as by local traffic. Nowadays, apart from occasional use by local farmers, they are havens of peace and quietness, left for walkers to enjoy. The drystone walls which bound many of them are likely, however, to be of fairly recent origin, products of enclosure around the end of the eighteenth and the beginning of the nineteenth centuries.

From Horton in Ribblesdale the Pennine Way follows such a green road which runs along the eastern flank of Ribblesdale in a northerly direction, roughly parallel with and near to the upper edge of the Great Scar Limestone. Several pot-holes can be found by the side of this road, formed by streams coming off the overlaying shale which have found their way underground down crevices in the limestone. Sell Gill Hole, which has openings on both sides of the road to form a natural bridge, has a pitch 150 ft (46 m) high and a huge chamber said to be one of the largest in the Dales; Pen-y-ghent Long Churn, further along, has a first pitch of 90 ft (27 m); and a third pot-hole, Red Moss Pot, has no

The final climb of Day 7: Pen-y-ghent

83

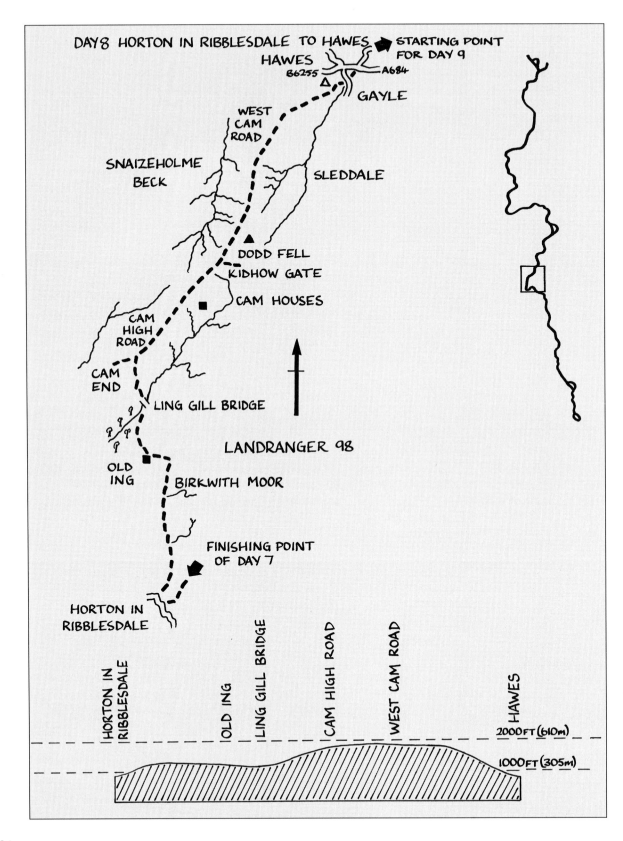

DAY 8 HORTON IN RIBBLESDALE TO HAWES
HAWES

STARTING POINT FOR DAY 9

B6255

A684

GAYLE

WEST CAM ROAD

SNAIZEHOLME BECK

SLEDDALE

DODD FELL

KIDHOW GATE

CAM HOUSES

CAM HIGH ROAD

CAM END

LING GILL BRIDGE

LANDRANGER 98

OLD ING

BIRKWITH MOOR

FINISHING POINT OF DAY 7

HORTON IN RIBBLESDALE

HORTON IN RIBBLESDALE

OLD ING

LING GILL BRIDGE

CAM HIGH ROAD

WEST CAM ROAD

HAWES

2000FT (610m)

1000FT (305m)

surface stream, but water can be heard running underground.

Around Birkwith Moor the Pennine Way leaves the green road—which continues on its journey into Langstrothdale—and goes eastwards towards the farm of Old Ing. Birkwith Moor was enclosed in 1758, so the walls on the right of the lane going up the moor are over two hundred years old. One of the privileges lost by enclosure was the Right of Turbary—the right to cut peat—and compensation or special provision was sometimes made for this. Black Dub Moss, an enclosed area a short distance from the Way, was given over to those who lost this right on Horton Moor. Old Ing goes back to at least the sixteenth century for it is mentioned in the will of one Anthony Proctor who, endeavouring to be fair to both his two sons, left his property to one on condition that the other received compensation of £20.

About a mile (1.6 km) north of Old Ing the Way crosses Ling Gill Beck. This stream rises as Cam Beck, becomes Ling Gill Beck a little lower down and then Cam Beck again just before it joins the Ribble. The origin of its name is uncertain, but it may derive from the use of the stream for retting the flax which was produced around here in the fourteenth century. At Ling Gill

Ling Gill Bridge

85

Above: Cam End

Opposite: The West Cam Road

the stream flows through a superb limestone gorge which is now protected as a National Nature Reserve. The mixed deciduous woodland which cloaks its sides is one of the few surviving scraps of the great forest which once covered large areas of the Yorkshire Dales. Destroyed by man and prevented from regeneration by grazing, it survives in only a few localities where some protection—natural or otherwise—has been given.

Ling Gill Bridge, which crosses the beck at the head of the gill, is a beautiful old stone packhorse bridge, important enough for its history to be recorded on a stone tablet on one of its parapets:

ANNO 1765
THIS BRIDGE
WAS REPAIR
ED AT THE
CHARGE OF
THE WHOLE W
EST RIDEING

The original bridge, which needed repairing by the eighteenth century, was built some two hundred years earlier at the expense of John Sigeswicke of Cam, who left forty shillings in his will to pay for it.

At Cam End, a short rise from Ling Gill Bridge, the Way joins the Cam High Road, a beautiful grassy track which climbs slowly for about 2½ miles (4 km) to its highest point around Kidhow Gate. This was originally a Roman road which ran south-west from the fort of Virosidum at Bainbridge over the high ground of Cam Fell into the head of Ribblesdale. Although most Roman roads were built in dead-straight lines, Roman engineers never hesitated to take a more roundabout and longer route if the local terrain demanded it, as for example in mountainous country. Clearly they thought it did here, for beyond Kidhow Gate the road departs markedly from a straight line and takes a southerly curve which avoids Dodd Fell and the head of Sleddale.

William Wilberforce, that great fighter against slavery and the slave trade, came along the Cam High Road in 1779 on a journey from Cambridge, where he was an undergraduate, to the Lake District and found it bleak and exposed. The lonely inn of Gearstones, situated where the road reaches the head of the Ribble Valley, was an important market for drove cattle attended by graziers and butchers. Some of these drove herds would certainly have come over the Cam High Road, for it linked up near Bainbridge with the great drove road which came

from Scotland and down the valley of the South Tyne.

From Cam End to Kidhow Gate the Cam High Road climbs slowly, keeping just below the crest of the hillside. A beautiful grassy way which is a delight to follow on a fine summer's day. In winter, when conditions are severe, it can be a different story. In the exceptionally bad winter of 1946–7 one holding of sheep was reduced in strength from a total of 600 when the winter began to only ninety at its end. South of the Cam High Road is the broad moorland valley of Cam Beck, now partly afforested, which contains the lonely farm of Cam Houses. There has been a settlement at Cam Houses for at least 800 years for it is mentioned in a document dated 1190. Wilberforce in 1779 dismissed it as 'five or six shabby huts', the only buildings he passed in 15 or 16 miles (24–27 km).

At Kidhow Gate the Way leaves the Roman road and turns in a more northerly direction, along another outstanding green road which cuts across the western flanks of Dodd Fell where they fall steeply into the deep valley of Snaizeholme. This is the West Cam Road, which runs for about 2½ miles (4 km) without changing appreciably either its direction or its height.

At the most northerly point of Dodd Fell where it narrows to a thin ridge, in an area of shake holes and old peat workings, the Pennine Way leaves the West Cam Road—which descends steeply into Snaizeholme—and takes a more gentle route in a north-easterly direction down a broad ridge. On the descent Hawes and Gayle come into view, set in the broad green sweep of Wensleydale. Gayle is a small village to the south of Hawes, although nowadays the two communities are virtually one. It is unfortunate that the Pennine Way passes it by, for it is a charming place with narrow alleys, seventeenth- and eigh-teenth-century cottages, a Sandemanian Chapel and mill built in 1784 which was used successively for cotton, flax and wool.

The final hundred yards (90 m) or so into Hawes is along a lovely flagged path called Bealer Bank; one of the ways used by packhorses as they came into the town. The modern factory over to the left of the Bank is the Wensleydale Creamery, the home of delicious white Wensleydale cheese. Bealer Bank leads to Hawes church and graveyard and to the main street of the town, which is entered through an arch. Hawes Youth Hostel, a modern purpose-built building with accommodation for sixty and opened in 1973, is at the far end of the main street on the Ingleton road. All things in their own time, however. Most walkers are likely to stop first—depending upon their inclination—at one of the many inns or cafés near by.

Gayle

DAY 9

THE CROSSING OF GREAT SHUNNER FELL:
Hawes to Keld

STARTING POINT
Hawes (98-873898)
FINISHING POINT
Keld (92-892010)
LENGTH
13 miles (21 km)
ASCENT
2150 ft (660 m)
TERRAIN
A long climb to the summit of Great
Shunner Fell followed by a long
descent into Swaledale. The final part
of the day is along a shelf overlooking
the upper reaches of the Swale.
REFRESHMENTS
A hotel/public house at Hardraw very
early in the day; also a café at
Thwaite.
ACCOMMODATION
A Youth Hostel and guest house at
Keld.

'. . . on Saturday morning went before Breakfast to see Hardrow Scar about a mile & ½ off. It is a Waterfall of the same kind as Whitfell and Mill Gills, but the fall is much greater, & the Rocks at the side higher . . .'

William Wilberforce, *Journey to the Lake District from Cambridge*
1779

Unlike most of the towns and villages in the northern part of the Yorkshire Dales, Hawes is of comparatively recent origin. There was some sort of settlement there in 1307, but it was still small three hundred years later and did not receive a Market Charter until 1700. (Wensley had one in 1202 and Askrigg in 1587.) The granting of the Charter was probably an indication that its importance was increasing, but it was the coming of the Lancaster to Richmond turnpike in 1795, followed by the railway in 1878, that led to the growth of Hawes as a major centre. Today, it is the second largest town in Wensleydale. For Pennine Way walkers it is a tempting place to linger, for the next villages of any size, Bowes and Middleton in Teesdale, are about two days' march away across bleak and lonely moors.

The way out of Hawes passes the site of the old railway station; this originally linked together two lines: a branch line from Garsdale run by the Midland Railway Company and one from Leyburn run by the North Eastern Railway Company. After closure in 1964 the station buildings and track rapidly deteriorated until the National Park Authority took them over. The main building is now a National Park Centre which houses a small exhibition on dales life.

Beyond the station the Way crosses the River Ure over a sturdy two-arched bridge and then follows paved paths —Hawes is noted for them—to the small hamlet of Hardrow.

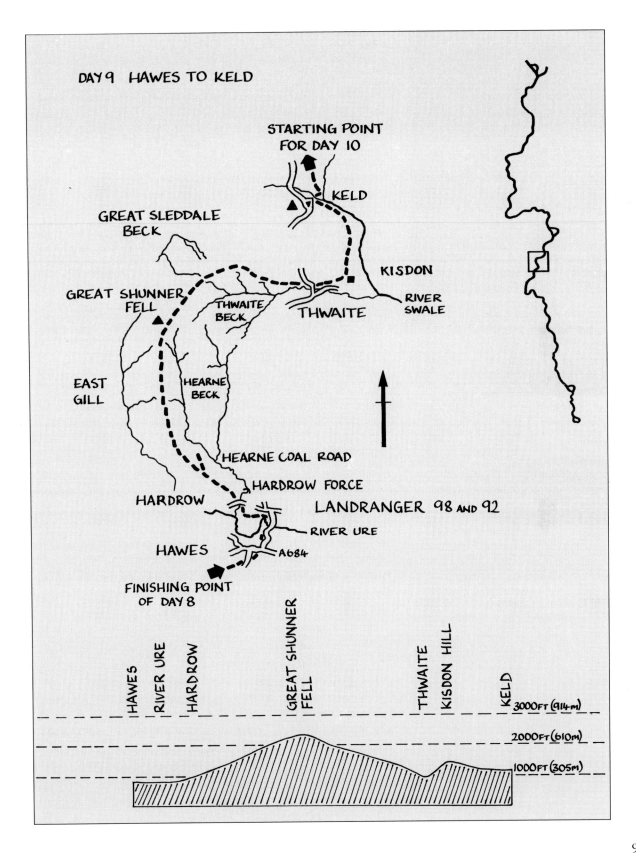

DAY 9 HAWES TO KELD

STARTING POINT
FOR DAY 10

KELD

GREAT SLEDDALE
BECK

KISDON

GREAT SHUNNER
FELL

THWAITE
BECK

RIVER
SWALE

THWAITE

EAST
GILL

HEARNE
BECK

HEARNE COAL ROAD

HARDROW FORCE

LANDRANGER 98 AND 92

HARDROW

RIVER URE

HAWES

A684

FINISHING POINT
OF DAY 8

HAWES
RIVER URE
HARDROW
GREAT SHUNNER FELL
THWAITE
KISDON HILL
KELD

3000FT (914m)

2000FT (610m)

1000FT (305m)

Hardrow Force in summer

One of the products taken by the new railway from Hawes was slates produced in quarries at Hardrow and nearby Simonstone. These were not true slates, but flags of sandstone from the Yoredale series of rocks. Although the slates were quarried at a number of places in the Yorkshire Dales, those from Hardrow were considered to be of the finest quality. First used in the seventeenth century, flag roofs are now a common feature on old cottages throughout the dales.

Most visitors to Hardrow, however, come to see the Force. This is a magnificent waterfall which drops over an overhanging lip of limestone into a plunge pool 95 ft (29 m) below. Erosion of soft shales beneath the limestone has produced a long recession gorge with steep, tree-covered sides. A favourite with the Victorian tourists who came to Hawes after the opening of the railway, its popularity was greatly enhanced in 1885 when a brass-band contest was held within the ravine. This was so successful that these contests became an annual event until the end of the century. They were revived for a time in the 1920s and again recently, but are not held at present. Visitors however, can still see the small bandstand and the tiered seats cut into the hillside for spectators. Those with no interest in brass-band contests would perhaps have appreciated more the feat of the great Blondin, who walked across Hardrow on a tight-rope, only stopping to cook an omelette in the middle! In exceptionally cold winters the fall has frozen completely to form a pillar of ice.

Owing to the dip of the strata in a northerly direction, the Great Scar Limestone, which was at a height of 1200 ft (365 m) on Pen-y-ghent, is almost completely concealed in Wensleydale and makes its appearance only on the floor of the dale as, for example, at Aysgarth where it is responsible for a fine series of falls. Wensleydale is cut, therefore, into the rocks of the Yoredale series, 1000 ft (305 m) thick, which consists of repeated sequences of limestones, sandstones, shales and thin coals. The long climb of the Way out of Hardrow towards the summit of Great Shunner Fell must cross these rock bands until the millstone grit cap is reached. The effect is a succession of steep sections separated by more gentle ones.

The climb from Hardrow to the summit is nearly 5 miles (8 km) long and involves a rise of 1570 ft (478 m). On a fine summer day this is a lovely moorland walk in which the uphill progress is barely noticed. Essentially it is a walk to be enjoyed for itself for there is little else to arouse excitement. Numerous cairns—described variously on Ordnance Survey maps as cairns, 'piles of stones', 'beacons' and even 'currack' (the last from the Old Welsh *carrecc*, meaning 'rock')—are passed on the

PENNINE SHEEP

The combination of high altitude with a cold climate, a short growing season and thin soil cover, largely determines the agriculture of the Pennines. With the exception of forestry, arable crops are almost entirely excluded, leaving the emphasis firmly on the grazing of sheep and cattle. Dairy herds are the mainstay of farms within the dales themselves and many hill farms will keep a few store cattle during the summer months. But as the altitude increases sheep come into their own.

Above and below: The hardy Swaledale breed

Of all breeds in the Pennines the Swaledale is probably the most common. First raised on the harsh moors in the northern part of the Yorkshire Dales, it has been much improved by selective breeding and has now spread to all parts of the Pennines, where its hardiness is much appreciated. It is a medium-sized sheep, with a black face and grey muzzle and strongly curving horns.

The Scotch Blackface is probably the most numerous and valuable breed in the United Kingdom, although losing some ground in the Pennines to the Swaledale. Slightly smaller than the Swaledale, this strongly horned sheep is distinguished by its black face and legs (sometimes mottled).

As its name implies, the Dalesbred is a breed of the Yorkshire Dales produced originally by crossing Scotch Blackface with Swaledale, but it is now a breed in its own right. Another black-faced sheep with curving horns, its main distinguishing features are the white patches on each side of the nose.

The Cheviot, a sheep first raised on the Border hills north of the Pennines, has now split into two types: the Hill or South Country Cheviot and the North Country Cheviot. The white, slightly arched faces and erect ears distinguish both from other breeds and the greater size and longer face of the North Country type from the other.

Other breeds may be met with on the Pennine Way. The Derbyshire Gritstone, a slightly disproportionate sheep with large body and small hornless head which is found in the Peak District; the Rough Fell, a large sheep with a long, straight fleece; and the Lonk, a compact type with a short, dense fleece. In addition to the raising of pure-bred sheep, it is common practice to cross ewes of the mountain and moorland types with rams noted for their greater body size, such as Teeswater, Wensleydale or Blue-faced Leicester, to produce crossbreeds (known as Mashams, Mules and Greyfaces) which are raised on lowland farms.

way. The thin seams of coal found in the Yoredale series were worked on Great Shunner Fell, as on Fountains Fell further to the south, and the remains of the workings occur by the track as you climb—until around 1950 ft (590 m) where the series gives way to millstone grit. A wide track, leaving the Way early in the climb, is the Hearne Coal Road which carried coal dug from the moor to local farms and villages.

It is likely that the name of Great Shunner Fell is a tribute both to its size and to the quality of its summit as a superb view-point, for it is probably derived from the Old Norse *sión* meaning 'view'. The summit is a good point for a rest, a drink and a bite to eat while you soak in the magnificence of the moorland scenery around you, secure in the knowledge that the descent should be comparatively painless. Four miles (6.5 km) of easy descent in a great curve between the headwaters of Thwaite Beck and Great Sleddale Beck will bring you to Thwaite, in Swaledale.

Walkers at this point will · be dismayed to discover the absence of a public house in Thwaite—or indeed at any point nearer than Muker down dale, which is an unacceptable 3 miles (5 km) there and back. (There is even worse to follow, for the same lack of a hostelry afflicts Keld, where the overnight stop is made.) There is, however, the Kearton Guest House which will supply teas. Thwaite was the birthplace of Cherry and Richard Kearton; both of whom were naturalists and lecturers of considerable merit and Cherry was also a pioneer of wildlife photography.

One last climb remains before the day's work is finished; up the steep slope behind the village to the farm of Kisdon. A splendid way, giving the opportunity to see over the length of Swaledale and compare its narrowness and roughness with the broad and green freshness of Wensleydale. An old way crosses the Pennine Way in the area of Kisdon along which corpses were taken in wicker coffins from the upper dales villages to the nearest consecrated ground, at Grinton; in extreme cases a journey of about 15 miles (24 km). By Kisdon there is also an old kiln—of which many hundreds exist in the dales—where local limestone and coal were burned to produce the lime needed to sweeten the fields.

Beyond Kisdon the Way runs along a superb shelf on the eastern flank of Kisdon Hill where it drops away steeply towards the river. For lovers of upper Swaledale—and there are many who think that there is nothing to compare with it—this is a walk with the gods. At the end of it is a final wood, a short lane and the hamlet of Keld. Rest well, for tomorrow is a big day—the arrival at Tan Hill Inn.

Above: Swaledale from Kisdon Hill

Opposite: Great Shunner Fell

DAY 10

THE STAINMORE GAP:
Keld to Baldersdale

STARTING POINT
Keld (91/92-892010)
FINISHING POINT
Baldersdale (91/92-932183)
LENGTH
15 miles (24 km)
ASCENT
1500 ft (460 m)
TERRAIN
Fairly featureless moorland with no
climbs of any note.
REFRESHMENTS
A hotel/public house (Tan Hill Inn)
reached about midday. Hotel/public
houses and cafés at Bowes on the
alternative route.
ACCOMMODATION
Youth Hostel in Baldersdale. Hotel/
public houses and guest houses in
Bowes area.

'IN MEMORY OF SUSAN PEACOCK WHO DIED 24 MAY
1937. LIVED HERE FROM 1902.'

Inscription on rockface, Tan Hill Inn

The lower part of Swaledale—around Grinton, Fremington,
Reeth and Healaugh—was settled early in the seventh century
by Anglo-Saxon invaders coming in from the east. The upper
dale beyond Feetham, however, was not colonized until the
tenth century, by Norsemen who came into the area from
Ireland. Gunnerside was a pasture used in spring by Gunnar for
the grazing of his cattle, Thwaite was an area cleared from the
forest, Muker a narrow field and Feetham the river meadow.
Common names, such as fell, beck, gill, moss, mere, crag and
clint, are also Norse in origin. It is very likely too that the dialect
of the Yorkshire Dales—so baffling to outsiders—owes
something to the language of the Norsemen.

Keld was originally Appeltreekeld, 'the spring near the apple
tree'. Despite the lack of a hostelry, there is no better place to
spend a night along the length of the Pennine Way than this
lovely village, the highest in Swaledale and the last before the
crossing of bleak and lonely Stainmore. Miners from the local
lead mines and smelt mills and from the coal pits around Tan
Hill have lived at Keld, but its greatest affinity has always been
with the land, and it is the shepherd, gathering his sheep from
the local fells or taking them to market along a dales road, who
has been most at one with his surroundings. There was never
very much at Keld, but the presence of two chapels testifies to
the strength of faith that must have been nurtured there.

From Keld the Pennine Way crosses the Swale near Kisdon
Force—a waterfall formed where the river flows over one of
the higher limestone bands of the Yoredale series—and heads
northwards along the western flank of Black Moor, parallel to
the road through West Stones Dale and by the lonely farms of
Low and High Frith. Tan Hill Inn is at the far end of the dale,

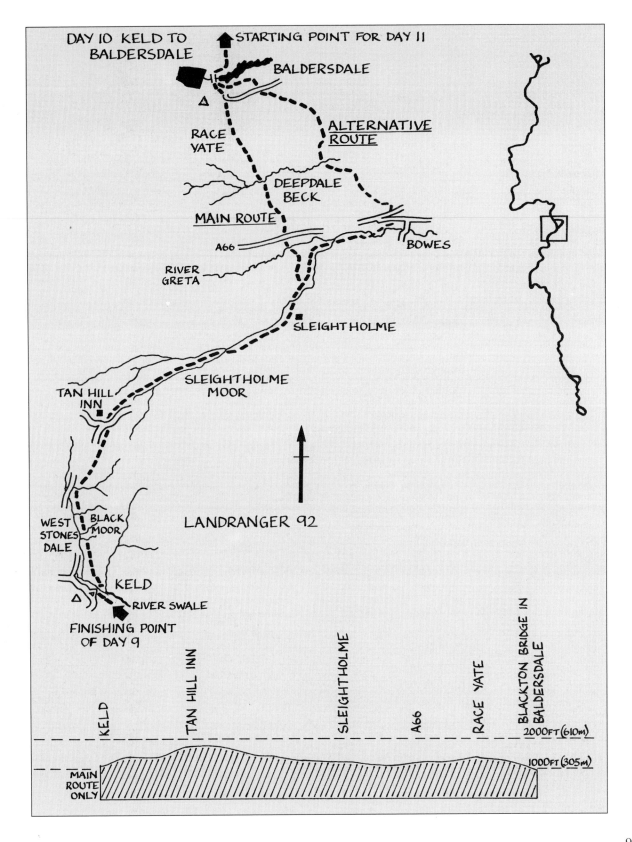

DAY 10 KELD TO BALDERSDALE

STARTING POINT FOR DAY 11

BALDERSDALE

RACE YATE

ALTERNATIVE ROUTE

DEEPDALE BECK

MAIN ROUTE

A66

BOWES

RIVER GRETA

SLEIGHTHOLME

SLEIGHTHOLME MOOR

TAN HILL INN

LANDRANGER 92

WEST STONES DALE

BLACK MOOR

KELD

RIVER SWALE

FINISHING POINT OF DAY 9

KELD

TAN HILL INN

SLEIGHTHOLME

A66

RACE YATE

BLACKTON BRIDGE IN BALDERSDALE

2000FT (610m)

1000FT (305m)

MAIN ROUTE ONLY

where the boundaries of Cumbria, Durham and North Yorkshire meet.

This isolated inn—claimed to be the highest in Britain (1732 ft/528 m)—is a welcome sight to Pennine Way travellers. Most of the glory of Tan Hill Inn, however, belongs to the past when it lay at the crossing point of important packhorse trails and at the centre of an intensive coal-mining area. As on Fountains Fell, the main coal seam lay just beneath the cap of millstone grit, with a second thinner and poorer one below in the higher layers of the Yoredale series. Extraction was carried out by the driving of levels into the seam or by the digging of vertical bell–pits. Tan Hill coal was used as long ago as the thirteenth and fourteenth centuries to warm the castles at Richmond and Appleby, but the real heyday came in the eighteenth and nineteenth centuries when it was used in local smelt mills. Few signs of this mining activity can now be seen—there are some shafts near to the Pennine Way as it approaches over Stonesdale Moor—but the old ways are still much in evidence as metalled roads or fine footpaths which radiate out from the inn in all directions.

At Tan Hill Inn the Pennine Way leaves the Yorkshire Dales National Park and begins the crossing at the Stainmore Gap. Walter Scott referred to 'Stanmore's shapeless swell', an apt description of the featureless moorland—the product of ice flow which smoothed its contours and smothered them in a thick blanket of boulder clay—between West Sleddale and Baldersdale. Although reaching a height of 1467 ft (447 m), the Gap offers a relatively easy passage through the Pennines which has been in continuous use for at least 3500 years. There is evidence of an ancient trade route of 1500 BC across the Gap, along which brass and gold ornaments were carried, and the Romans built a road there with forts at Bowes and Brough during the time of Agricola in the first century AD, as part of their campaign to subdue the tribe of the Brigantes. Normans built castles there and Scottish raiders used it during their pillages of the fourteenth century.

The Gap was also the scene in AD 954 of the Battle of Stainmore in which Eric Bloodaxe, son of Harold Fairhair and the last Viking king of Northumbria, was defeated and slain. Present-day use of the Stainmore Gap is considerably tamer than in the past and is largely confined to the A66, Scotch Corner-Penrith road, which runs along the line of the old Roman road. A railway line was opened over Stainmore in 1861 by the South Durham & Lancashire Union Railway; at the turn

A corner of Keld

Right: The most famous of all Pennine
Way watering holes: Tan Hill Inn

of the century it was a busy line carrying iron ore and coal over
the Pennines, but declining work forced its closure in 1962.

After the lonely moors of the Stainmore Gap the crossing of
the A66 is both noisy and unpleasant. Those who wish to avoid
crossing here can do so by taking the alternative route which
goes further to the east into Bowes. This was included to give
accommodation in the days before Baldersdale Youth Hostel
was opened. The extra distance is not insignificant—about 4½
miles (7 km)—but Bowes is an interesting place with a fair
range of accommodation (an ideal place for a rest day for those
now in need of one!). The Roman fort of Lavatrae, which
guarded the eastern end of the Gap, is at Bowes. A churchyard
occupies the north-east corner and the Norman castle the
north-west, but the rampart-mound of the fort can be made out
on two sides. Dotheboys Hall in *Nicholas Nickleby* was modelled
by Charles Dickens on a school in Bowes run by William Shaw
which he visited in 1838. Whatever the justification for
Dickens's portrayal—Shaw was probably no worse than many
other owners of similar establishments—predictably it brought
about a sharp reduction in the number of children sent to the
boarding schools of Bowes!

The final stretch along the main route—about 4 miles (6.5
km) after the crossing of the A66—is easy stuff, even though
the valley of Deep Dale lies in the way (it is only deep by
Stainmore standards, not by those of other parts). The final mile
(1.6 km) or so, from beyond Race Yate, is all downhill.

Without doubt, Day 10 is one to be remembered. Not for the
scenery, though, which is on the whole not worth writing home
about. Nor for features of interest, for apart from Tan Hill Inn
there are few. The event which makes this day special is the
arrival at Blackton Bridge in Baldersdale, generally considered to
be the half-way point of the Pennine Way.

Opposite: Bowes Castle

DAY 11

TEESDALE:
Baldersdale to Langdon Beck

STARTING POINT
Baldersdale (91/92-932183)
FINISHING POINT
Langdon Back (91/92-853312)
LENGTH
15 miles (24 km)
ASCENT
1300 ft (400 m)
TERRAIN
Easy walking across fields and semi-moorland leads to Middleton-in-Teesdale; thereafter, superb path alongside the Tees.
REFRESHMENTS
Hotel/public houses, cafés and shops at Middleton-in-Teesdale.
ACCOMMODATION
Youth Hostel and hotel/public house at Langdon Beck.

'For men may come and men may go,
But I go on for ever.'

Alfred Lord Tennyson, 'The Brook'

The Youth Hostel at Baldersdale was originally a farmhouse, Blackton Farm, built from stone in traditional dales style. Bought as an Outdoor Pursuits Centre, it was available for sale again in spring 1977, when it was purchased by the Youth Hostels Association aided by the Department of Education and Science. Conversion was carried out with the assistance of the Countryside Commission. It lies a short distance off the Way, beneath the towering dam of Baldersdale Reservoir. Before the hostel was opened in spring 1981, non-camping walkers had to push on to Middleton-in-Teesdale, leaving a short following day to reach the hostel at Langdon Beck.

The farm of Low Birk Hat in Baldersdale was the home for many years of Hannah Hauxwell, who became famous through the television programme *Too Long a Winter,* which was broadcast by Yorkshire Television in 1973, and the book *Hannah in Yorkshire.*

The way from Baldersdale to Middleton-in-Teesdale is an easy walk across meadows, rough pastures and rather marshy semi-moorland broken by enclosure walling. The broad, shallow valley of Lunedale is crossed at about the half-way point using the five-arch stone bridge which spans the western end of Grassholme Reservoir. Baldersdale and Lunedale are quiet, lonely dales dotted with numerous small farmhouses, but with no villages of any note until Teesdale is reached. This is lapwing country—unlike the high moors, which are curlew country—and the best time to come here is in spring, when the males indulge the females with their wild, flamboyant aerial displays. Appropriately, the lapwing was chosen as the emblem of the Baldersdale Youth hostel.

On the way down into Middleton the Way goes near to the

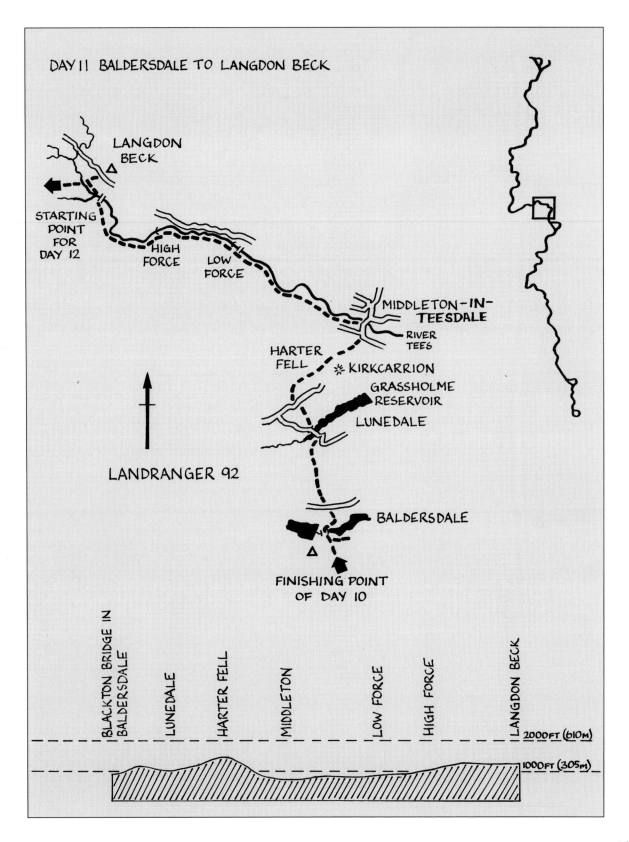

DAY 11 BALDERSDALE TO LANGDON BECK

LANGDON BECK

STARTING POINT FOR DAY 12

HIGH FORCE

LOW FORCE

MIDDLETON-IN-TEESDALE

RIVER TEES

HARTER FELL

※ KIRKCARRION

GRASSHOLME RESERVOIR

LUNEDALE

LANDRANGER 92

BALDERSDALE

FINISHING POINT OF DAY 10

BLACKTON BRIDGE IN BALDERSDALE

LUNEDALE

HARTER FELL

MIDDLETON

LOW FORCE

HIGH FORCE

LANGDON BECK

2000FT (610M)

1000FT (305M)

LEAD MINING IN THE PENNINES

With some minor exceptions the lead ore which was mined in the Pennines was galena or lead sulphide. This occurs in veins with other materials, such as fluorspar and barytes, known collectively as gangue. The major veins run vertically, up to 20 ft (6 m) wide, over 500 ft (150 m) deep and usually a mile (1.6 km) or so in length. Many veins, however, are much narrower and some deposits also occur in horizontal layers and irregular masses. Even within a vein the galena content is low—usually about 5%—although the percentage of lead finally obtained is nearly the same.

It is certain that mining was carried out during the Roman occupation, as lead pigs of that period have been found in the Yorkshire Dales and the Peak District, and may have pre-dated the Romans. Mining probably continued after they left, through the Dark Ages and the Norman Conquest—Domesday Book, for example, records several smelting sites in the Peak District—and in the Tudor period. The most productive years of the industry, however, were during the Industrial Revolution, in the late-eighteenth and early-nineteenth centuries. Mines were worked in the White Peak area of Derbyshire, around Swaledale and near Grassington in the Yorkshire Dales and further north on Alston Moor to the north of Cross Fell.

In the very early days extraction was carried out by the open-cast working of veins coming to the surface, but later was accomplished from shafts dug along the line of a vein from which horizontal levels were driven. In some cases levels were also driven horizontally into a vein from a nearby hillside. Drainage was often a problem, particularly as shafts and levels approached the water table. Although mechanical devices were used from the earliest days to overcome this difficulty, the most important development was the use of soughs—long drainage tunnels—which were driven from a mine to a convenient valley. From early in the eighteenth century steam engines were used for pumping. After extraction the ore was crushed and separated before smelting.

The exhaustion of some of the larger veins, the difficulties with drainage and the low price of lead due to overseas competition were some of the factors that caused a rapid decline in the second half of the nineteenth century. Although attempts have been made this century to revive small workings, these have been short-lived and the industry is therefore now a thing of the past.

Old Gang Smelt Mill

prominent wooded hilltop of Kirkcarrion, where a Bronze Age burial mound was excavated in 1804, and later crosses the line of a superb holloway which runs across the hillsides to the south of the Tees.

Middleton is the capital of Upper Teesdale; a substantial village with shops, restaurants, inns and guesthouses. Try to reach it in time for lunch. The heyday of Middleton came in the nineteenth century when part of it was owned by the London Lead Company, which operated mines in the dale. Unlike most employers at that time, the Quaker-based company had a genuine interest in the welfare of its workers and built houses and provided numerous services, such as a library, health centre, public washhouses and evening classes. One relic of those times is the cast-iron fountain in the centre of the village, erected in 1877 in commemoration of a testimonial presented to Robert Bainbridge, a company superintendent.

Despite its attractions, it is best not to linger too long in Middleton for there are still several miles to go to Langdon Beck; miles, moreover, which follow the Tees through some of its finest stretches. Not that this is apparent immediately—or indeed for some time—for the Way keeps fairly clear of the river for the first mile or two (1.6–3km) after Middleton, taking a sensible line to the south, which avoids a whole series of otherwise irritating and time-consuming meanders. When the Tees adopts a straighter course, then the Way comes to it and keeps it company nearly all the way to Langdon Beck. The pleasant green fields of Teesdale are the first—in any quantity—since the Aire Gap many miles and days ago. They should be enjoyed.

The dominating influence of Upper Teesdale—as it is further north along Hadrian's Wall—is the series of highly resistant dolerite bands of the Whin Sill which outcrop along its length. The spectacular waterfalls of Low and High Force, the magnificent cascade of Cauldron Snout and the dark, brooding crags of Cronkley Scar and Falcon Clints all owe their existence to it. All of these can be seen to perfection from view-points along the Way, either on this day or early on the next.

In any other setting, Low Force—a series of picturesque falls—would be considered worth visiting in its own right; on the Way, however, it is but a prelude to greater glories and it is its much bigger brother which will be remembered the best. At High Force the Tees falls in a single magnificent leap of about 65

Previous page: Middleton-in-Teesdale

Right: Low Force

ft (20 m) over the edge of the Whin Sill into a deep plunge pool. As the resistant dolerite rests on more easily eroded limestone, progressive collapse has taken place, leading to the formation of a deep recession gorge. Normally, there is only one fall on the south side, but a second, separated from the first by a column of rock, opens up in very wet weather. It is said that in extremely unusual conditions in the past the entire rock edge has been covered, and on some occasions the fall has frozen solid. Pennine Way walkers enjoy the sight free of charge, those seen on the opposite bank have had to pay for the privilege.

Surmounting a small, juniper-clothed hill, there can be seen ahead the scatter of whitewashed houses and farms which form Forest-in-Teesdale. Although the valley is 1000 ft (300 m) high, settlement goes back to the earliest times. Axes used by Neolithic farmers have been found there, and in Teesdale Cave, located in a scar on the north side of the valley, the bones of an Iron Age woman were discovered in the late-eighteenth century along with the remains of wolf and lynx. Much later there was a smelting mill and a lead mine situated there.

Nowadays, apart from the scattered farmsteads, there is comparatively little: a purpose-built Youth Hostel, the Langdon Beck Hotel—built in 1887 to replace an earlier inn—and a small church. There is, however, no other accommodation until Dufton and Pennine Way walkers would be wise to take every advantage of its excellent hospitality.

High Force

DAY 12

ACROSS THE PENNINES:
Langdon Beck to Dufton

STARTING POINT
Langdon Beck (91/92-853312)
FINISHING POINT
Dufton (91-690250)
LENGTH
14 miles (22 km)
ASCENT
800 ft (240 m)
TERRAIN
A superb walk alongside the Tees
finishing with a scramble up rocks by
Cauldron Snout; then a rough
moorland crossing, part of the way
following Maize Beck. Finally, a long
descent from High Cup.
REFRESHMENTS
None along the way. A hotel/public
house and a shop at Dufton.
ACCOMMODATION
Youth Hostel and guest houses at
Dufton.

'As planned the Pennine Way is approximately 250 miles in length. It does not seek the shortest distance between the two terminal points, but crosses first to one and then to the other side of the Pennines to link up numerous features of scenic or historic interest.'

Memorandum of the Pennine Way Association, 1942

From the beginning the Pennine Way was envisaged as both a high-level route and as a trail linking up places of natural beauty or historical or romantic interest. It was the need to reconcile these two requirements that accounts for the strange contortions of the Way between Bowes and Alston.

If the Way had been intended *exclusively* as a high-level route—and planned with total freedom—then a very demanding line could have been taken from the Stainmore Gap to the area of the Wall. Instead of this, however, the Pennine Way goes over to Middleton-in-Teesdale on the eastern side of the Pennines and then takes a route of only moderate difficulty, virtually due west, along Teesdale and the valley of Maize Beck, down to Dufton on the western side. A high-level traverse from Knock Fell to Cross Fell is included, but there is a soft finish along the valley of the South Tyne. Surely, however, the planners were right: missing out such gems as High Force, Cauldron Snout and High Cup would have been much too high a price to pay.

From Langdon Beck the Way goes in a westerly direction, cutting across low-lying pasture to rejoin the Tees about a mile (1.6 km) from its confluence with Harwood Beck. Although only a few miles from its source, the Tees is already very wide and provides a pleasant background of sound as it flows over its pebbly bed. The dark cliff on the opposite side of the river where the Pennine Way reaches it, is Cronkley Scar; another product of the Whin Sill. On Widdybank Fell, north of the river, soft, green Silurian slates were quarried during the

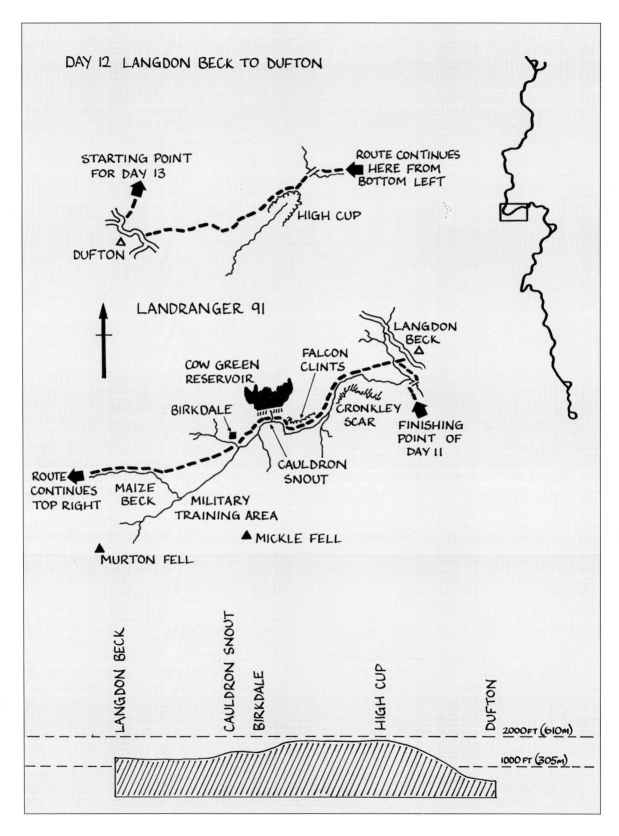

DAY 12 LANGDON BECK TO DUFTON

STARTING POINT
FOR DAY 13

ROUTE CONTINUES
HERE FROM
BOTTOM LEFT

HIGH CUP

DUFTON

LANDRANGER 91

LANGDON
BECK

COW GREEN
RESERVOIR

FALCON
CLINTS

BIRKDALE

CRONKLEY
SCAR

CAULDRON
SNOUT

FINISHING
POINT OF
DAY 11

ROUTE
CONTINUES
TOP RIGHT

MAIZE
BECK

MILITARY
TRAINING AREA

MICKLE FELL

MURTON FELL

LANGDON BECK

CAULDRON SNOUT

BIRKDALE

HIGH CUP

DUFTON

2000FT (610M)

1000 FT (305M)

nineteenth century to be made into pencils at a mill nearby.

The Way follows the Tees for 2½ miles (4 km) as it takes a great loop to the south, first over the gentle pastures of Holmwath and then later along a narrow, rough and rocky shelf beneath the dolerite scar of Falcon Clints. The journey along the Tees, which began yesterday, is now almost at an end, but this river has a great sense of occasion and—like all good actors—has left its greatest moment to last. Cauldron Snout, where the Tees comes down from the high moorland over the lip of the Whin Sill in a series of magnificent white cascades 200 ft (60 m) long, should receive a standing ovation. The river was mentioned in the Viking Knytlinga saga of 1026, where it was known as 'Tese' or 'the boiling, surging river'; this description fits Cauldron Snout better than any other place on the river and it may be there that the Viking storytellers had in mind. The Pennine Way climbs the rocks by the side of the Snout and crosses over to the far side of the Tees by a footbridge just below the massive dam of Cow Green Reservoir.

Upper Teesdale has long been recognized as an area of immense interest and importance, not just for the unique character of its geology and landforms, but also for its flora and fauna. It was very appropriate, therefore, that some measure of protection was given to it by the Nature Conservancy Council in the 1960s with the establishment of the Upper Teesdale National Nature Reserve. This covers an immense area of 8600 acres (3500 hectares) over Mickle, Cronkley and Widdybank Fells and includes the section of the Way between High Force and Cauldron Snout. No protection was given, however, to the area of the Tees north of the Snout, and the construction there between 1967 and 1970 of the Cow Green Dam resulted in the flooding of the Tees valley for over 2 miles (3 km). Although a strong case was made out for the extra water that the reservoir would supply and, when all was lost, action was taken to reduce the impact on local wildlife, the result can only be viewed as an environmental disaster.

A short distance beyond Cauldron Snout and the dam of the reservoir, the Way passes the small farm of Birkdale. Nowadays, Birkdale is a lonely place, the last habitation before the moorland crossing which takes the Way from Teesdale to the Eden valley. In the heyday of cattle droving, however, this farm lay on the great drove road which brought cattle down from the Southern Uplands, north of the Scottish border, to Malham and

Previous page: Falcon Clints

Left: The most dramatic view point in the Pennines: High Cup

Cauldron Snout

the Craven district of the Yorkshire Dales. The walled enclosures around the farm were used for the overnight pasturing of cattle, while the buildings provided shelter and hospitality for the drovers themselves. The herds came to Birkdale from the valley of the South Tyne to the north-west, leaving it again over a ford to the south and by a green track which went eastwards over Cronkley Fell to Holwick.

From Birkdale the Way crosses open moor for about 2 miles (3 km) until Maize Beck is rejoined. The area to the south is a military training ground, its boundary marked out by regularly spaced noticeboards. Spoil heaps at Moss Shop reveal the presence of an old lead mine, one of many in this area. Further along, Maize Beck can normally be forded, but the correct line of the Way follows the right bank of the stream to a footbridge higher up (this route is essential if the beck is high).

The featureless and apparently innocuous plain beyond Maize Beck is in reality a build-up to the most dramatic view-point in the Pennines. Not the slightest hint of this is given, however, and it is only in the final yards, when the level moor falls away with dramatic suddenness to reveal the magnificent valley of High Cup, that the overall pattern is perceived. No amount of anticipation can reduce the visual impact of that moment.

High Cup is a beautifully symmetrical, U-shaped valley, nearly 1½ miles (2.5 km) long and 660 ft (200 m) deep, a product of a glacier that gouged its way into the great western scarp of the Cross Fell massif during the Ice Age. The black cliffs exposed around the edge of the Cup are hard dolerite formed when the glacier cut down through the layer of the Whin Sill. Beyond High Cup are the green fields of the Vale of Eden and further still the Lakeland hills.

From the head of High Cup the Pennine Way continues on its way in a south-westerly direction along a level but narrow shelf above the northern line of cliff, appropriately called Narrow Gate. Along the way a drink can be obtained at Hannah's Well, which is not a well but a small spring. Soon the shelf broadens and the path goes down slopes until the first enclosure walls of the Eden valley are reached; during the descent the presence of limestone is marked by lines of shake holes which run along the hillside. The final mile (1.6 km) or so into Dufton is along a farm track and then a metalled road.

Dufton is a natural overnight stopping point, for there is no further accommodation until the South Tyne Valley, many miles and four mountain summits hence. For Pennine Way walkers there are several guest houses which will provide bed and breakfast, a Youth Hostel, an inn and a post office/shop. Who could ask for more?

DAY 13

THE ROOF OF THE PENNINES:
Dufton to Alston

'. . . to climb steep hills
Requires slow pace at first.'

William Shakespeare, *King Henry VIII*

Dufton, with its delightful green shadowed by rows of sturdy mature trees and surrounded by small cottages, is a haven after the bleak crossing from upper Teesdale. As usual in these small villages of the High Pennines, the devout are well catered for and there is both a Methodist Chapel, built in 1905, and—along the road towards Knock—the Church of St Cuthbert, which probably dates back to the twelfth century.

Not many years ago, youth hostellers arriving here along the Pennine Way had to travel on for a further mile or two towards Knock and then retrace their footsteps part of the way next morning. Nowadays, the hostel is in the centre of the village. Pennine Way walkers who stay there should be particularly pleased to see a picture of Tom Stephenson over the fireplace in the common room. There is also in the village the lovely little Stag Inn, just opposite the hostel, which will provide excellent hospitality.

The delights of Dufton are best sampled in the cool of a summer's evening and not on the morning of departure, for the day's walking from there to Alston is the longest of them all. It includes a traverse of Cross Fell, the highest point in the Pennines, and the highest in England outside the Lake District.

All the height lost on the previous afternoon during the long descent from High Cup has to be made up at the start of the day as the Way heads immediately towards the great escarpment, nearly 2000 ft (600 m) high, which forms the western face of the Cross Fell range. For the first mile (1.6 km) or so the climbing is fairly gentle as the Way takes an oblique route up the lower slopes between Knock Pike and Dufton Pike. Beyond

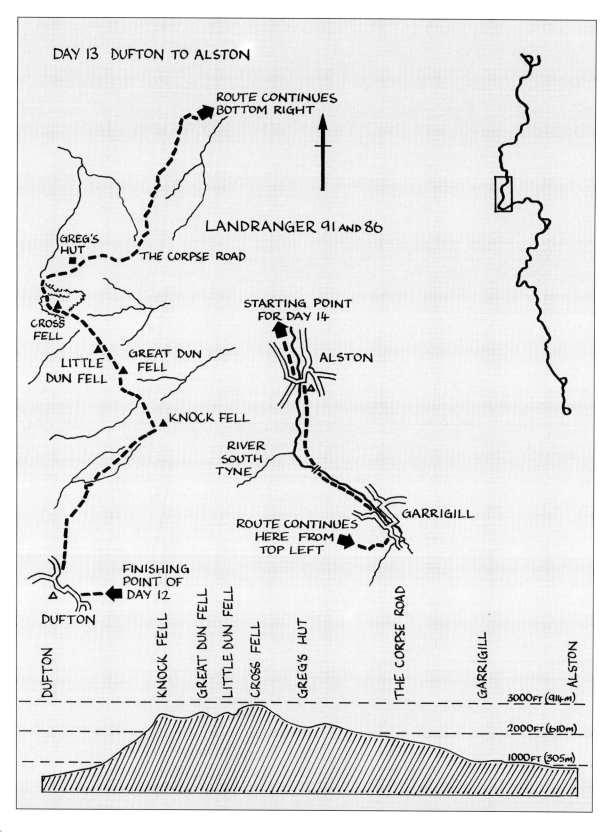

DAY 13 DUFTON TO ALSTON

ROUTE CONTINUES
BOTTOM RIGHT

LANDRANGER 91 AND 86

GREG'S
HUT

THE CORPSE ROAD

STARTING POINT
FOR DAY 14

CROSS
FELL

ALSTON

LITTLE
DUN FELL

GREAT DUN
FELL

KNOCK FELL

RIVER
SOUTH
TYNE

GARRIGILL

ROUTE CONTINUES
HERE FROM
TOP LEFT

FINISHING
POINT OF
DAY 12

DUFTON

DUFTON

KNOCK FELL

GREAT DUN FELL

LITTLE DUN FELL

CROSS FELL

GREG'S HUT

THE CORPSE ROAD

GARRIGILL

ALSTON

3000FT (914m)

2000FT (610m)

1000FT (305m)

Above: Clapper Bridge, Great Rundale
Beck

Previous page: The green at Dufton

Opposite: Greg's Hut on the Corpse
Road

Great Rundale Beck, however, which is crossed over a small
clapper bridge, the way becomes steeper as it moves over to a
more direct line. Altogether it is about 4 miles (6.5 km) of
continuous climbing from Dufton to the summit of Knock Fell.
It probably does not need saying, but the summit of Knock Fell
is an ideal place for the first rest of the day!

From Knock Fell the Way swings through ninety degrees and
commences a high-level traverse over the summits of Great and
Little Dun Fells and Cross Fell. In good weather this is a grand
walk with superb views down the steep western escarpment
over the Vale of Eden and into the blue haze of distant Lakeland
hills. In bad weather it is a fight against the elements, for the
ridge is exposed to the full fury of westerly winds. It is salutary
to remember that in January 1974 an hourly mean wind of 92
knots (106 mph) was recorded over Great Dun Fell, the highest
ever in Great Britain. This is also the area of the Helm Wind,
notorious for its violence, although this is a feature of the lower
slopes of the escarpment and the immediate lowland area
beneath it, rather than the ridge itself. It is thought to result
from the acceleration of east to north-east winds as they flow
down the steep western slopes. Its presence is revealed by a cap
of cloud (the 'Helm') over Cross Fell and a long bar of cloud
(the 'Helm Bar') about 5 miles (8 km) to the west.

Great Dun Fell has suffered some desecration by the erection
of buildings, masts and a radome. The earlier station here was
erected in the 1940s, but has recently been altered and
extended. It provides long-range radar and air-ground-air radio

facilities. The road which runs up to it offered a tempting alternative to Pennine Way travellers when the hostel was at Knock, leading frequently to a bypassing of Knock Fell. Nowadays, there is no excuse! Cross Fell is a great flat-topped mountain with numerous cairns and an Ordnance Survey obelisk, surrounded by small crags and scree slopes. In thick mist care is needed in its crossing.

The Way crosses the summit area and drops down on the far side to meet a track which comes up from Kirkland. For many years this track carried the dead of Garrigill, who had to be carried over to the nearest consecrated ground; hence it became known as the Corpse Road. The Pennine Way follows it on a long descent down Alston Moor to the small hamlet of Garrigill.

A short distance down on the Alston side the Way passes a small stone cottage with flagged roof situated on the open moor by a spoil heap. This was originally a miner's cottage, but was restored and opened as a mountain bothy in May 1972. In memory of John Gregory, who died in 1968 at the age of forty, it is known as Greg's Hut. It is a simple structure of two rooms, with fireplace, basic furniture and cooking equipment, for the benefit of travellers in need of shelter in this lonely spot.

There are other reminders of the lead-mining industry— spoil heaps, shafts and ruins—on the way down to Garrigill, for Alston Moor (formerly Aldenstane Moor) was an important mineral field. Perhaps most interesting are the blue crystals of fluorspar which litter the path, often finding their way into pockets and rucksacks as souvenirs of the journey.

Garrigill has a population of about two hundred, but it boasts two chapels—at Gate Head and Low Houses—and a church, all still in use. The spirit of the Good Samaritan is very much alive in Garrigill, for a notice in the church informs visitors that 'Sanctuary is gladly provided for walkers in severe weather, distress or genuine emergency . . .' There is also a post office, a store and a hotel. After the long descent from Cross Fell the green at Garrigill is extremely pleasant; an ideal place to relax for a while in the warmth of the late afternoon sunshine and exchange the latest gossip of the day with fellow-travellers.

The easiest part of this section comes—fortunately—at the end: about 3 miles (5 km) of easy walking along the banks of the South Tyne until Alston is reached. The Youth Hostel is situated right by the Way where it enters the town, the hotels and guesthouses are slightly further along. With Cross Fell safely out of the way and an easier day on the morrow, most walkers should sleep well in their beds tonight.

The highest summit: Cross Fell, looking back along the ridge to Great Dun Fell

DAY 14

APPROACH TO THE WALL:

Alston to Greenhead

STARTING POINT
Alston (86-719462)
FINISHING POINT
Greenhead (86-660654)
LENGTH
18 miles (29 km)
ASCENT
1650 ft (500 m)
TERRAIN
Follows the valley of the South Tyne, but generally avoids the river over moorland to the west. A long but fairly easy walk.
REFRESHMENTS
Shop at Slaggyford. A hotel/public house at Knarsdale.
ACCOMMODTION
Youth Hostel, hotel/public house and guest houses at Greenhead.

'And over the highways and byeways I plod,
My clothes are all tattered my feet are ill-shod,
But there isn't a roadway that I haven't trod,
Being forty-five summers a drover.'

Packie Manus Byrne, 'Life of a drover'

From Alston to Greenhead the Way follows the valley of the South Tyne, heading directly for the north—and for Hadrian's Wall. However, those expecting a repeat of the delightful river walk which they experienced further south along the Tees will be disappointed. There is one good stretch by the river, just south of Slaggyford, but that is all too brief and mostly the Way keeps well away from it, preferring instead to use the hillsides over to the west. After Lambley the two part company altogether, one swinging away directly eastwards, the other continuing to the north. In the main this is a fairly easy day with relatively little climbing and, frankly, not too many features of great interest. With the exertions of the Cross Fell range now happily behind and all the excitement of Hadrian's Wall to come on the morrow, this is essentially a day for recharging your batteries. A day for quiet enjoyment, while the miles slip by easily and almost unnoticed.

Alston, situated on a spur above the meeting point of the South Tyne and the Nent at an elevation of about 1080 ft (330 m), is the highest market town in England. Settlement probably goes back to at least Anglo-Saxon times, but the major development took place much later, during the growth of the lead-mining industry. It is the last major centre before Bellingham, three days hence, although some supplies can be picked up at Slaggyford and Greenhead.

The Pennine Way leaves Alston from the western end of the bridge over the river. There is a major diverson away from the

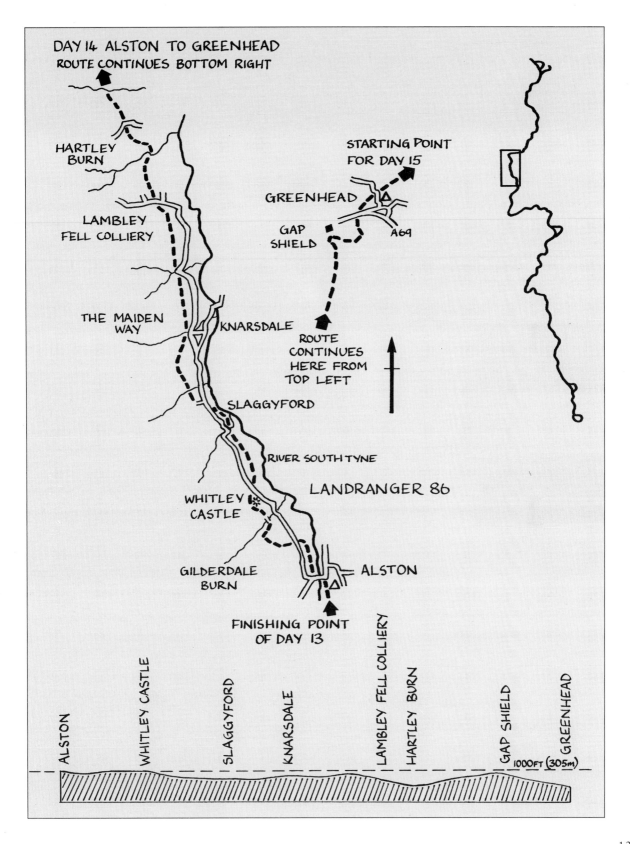

DAY 14 ALSTON TO GREENHEAD
ROUTE CONTINUES BOTTOM RIGHT

HARTLEY
BURN

LAMBLEY
FELL COLLIERY

THE MAIDEN
WAY

KNARSDALE

SLAGGYFORD

RIVER SOUTH TYNE

WHITLEY
CASTLE

GILDERDALE
BURN

FINISHING POINT
OF DAY 13

STARTING POINT
FOR DAY 15

GREENHEAD

GAP
SHIELD

A69

ROUTE
CONTINUES
HERE FROM
TOP LEFT

LANDRANGER 86

ALSTON

ALSTON

WHITLEY CASTLE

SLAGGYFORD

KNARSDALE

LAMBLEY FELL COLLIERY

HARTLEY BURN

GAP SHIELD

GREENHEAD

1000FT (305m)

valley almost immediately as the Way swings away to reach and
then cross the Gilderdale Burn. (Streams become burns in these
parts and cloughs become cleughs.) Although rough in places
and not easy to follow—despite some of the largest fingerposts
along the Way—it gets the walker away from the A689 and
into an excellent position to view the earthworks of Whitley
Castle. This is not a castle, but a fort on the Maiden Way, a
Roman road which ran between the forts of Bravoniacum (near
Kirkby Thorne) and Carvoran (on the Wall). The fort is situated
in a commanding position with useful views in both directions
up and down the valley and to neighbouring hills. It was
probably constructed to safeguard the road, which was an
important supply line to the Wall, and also for the protection of
local mine workings. Just before the fort, at a footbridge over
the Gilderdale Burn, the Way leaves Cumbria and enters
Northumberland, the last county before the crossing of the
border.

The South Tyne Valley from Gilsland to Alston lay along the
route of the great drove road which brought cattle down from
Scotland to the northern area of the Yorkshire Dales and
eventually further south. This road has been met before along
the Way, for it came past Birkdale and near Tan Hill Inn.

Towards the end of the morning walkers should reach
Slaggyford and then Knarsdale, which is about a mile (1.6 km)
further along. 'Slaggy' is derived from the Middle English word
'slag' which means 'slippery with mud', and hence Slaggyford is
'the muddy ford'; while Knarsdale is 'the valley by the rugged
rock'. Both are little more than hamlets, although the former
boasts a post office/store and the latter an inn. The morbid may
wish to make a detour to the churchyard in Knarsdale to see the
gravestone which marks the last resting place of Robert Baxter,
a local shepherd, who died on 4 October 1796 after eating some
food which he found on the moors. There was the suspicion of
foul play, as his gravestone relates:

All you that please these lines to read,
It will cause a tender heart to bleed;
I murdered was upon the fell,
And by the man I know full well;
By bread and butter which he'd laid,
I being harmless, was betrayed.
I hope he will rewarded be;
That laid the poison there for me.

Alston

OLD WAYS IN THE PENNINES: THE DROVE ROADS

Although some movement of cattle—for example, to new grazing grounds—had taken place since ancient times, the driving of great herds from one part of the country to another for the purposes of trade was largely a product of the seventeenth century. It is likely that the breakdown of the medieval system of land ownership was a factor in this development, as it encouraged the exchange of produce between upland villages and lowland areas. The main reason, however, was the rapid growth of many English towns, whose need for meat products soon exceeded what neighbouring country areas could supply.

Of particular importance was the trade between England and Scotland. Large numbers of cattle gathered from the Highlands, were driven over the border, to be fattened before they continued their journey further south. Great Close on Malham Moor was used as a pasture for fattening on which 5000 head could be grazed at one time.

A drover, with help from a boy and two or three dogs, would handle about forty or fifty head, but drovers would sometimes join together to form a herd up to 200 strong with a man for every forty beasts or so. The driving of a herd was a fairly leisurely business, for it was essential to keep the cattle in good condition. Twelve miles (19 km) each day, with regular stops for rest and food, was thought satisfactory. For easy movement the drovers usually chose to drive across open country away from towns, and preferred traditional green drovers' ways to the new turnpikes. Night would be spent in the open, or in greater comfort at a farm or one of the small inns on the routes.

Mastiles Lane, an old drove road near Malham Tarn

Although the eighteenth century was a time of prosperity for the droving trade, the following century saw its dramatic decline. The enclosure of upland areas, which robbed the drover of overnight grazing, the further development of turnpikes and later of the railways, and improved stock breeding in England were some of the factors involved.

The passage of over 150 years since the droving trade ceased has been insufficient to erase all signs of it from the Pennines. Place-names containing the words 'ox', 'drift' or 'drove' probably indicate that a drove road passed that way; some of the overnight stopping places, such as Gearstones near Ribblehead, with their surrounding patchwork of small enclosures, are still occupied; and broad green trails still offer good walking over rough moorland areas.

Drovers with their flock; both cattle and sheep were taken south

North of Knarsdale the Pennine Way follows the line of the Maiden Way—which can be detected in parts—as it crosses over spurs of moorland, into the valley of the Glendue Burn and then down to the A689 near Lambley. The long jagged edge, away towards the north-east, is the Whin Sill, which marks the line of Hadrian's Wall. Eighteen hundred years or so ago that sight must have warmed the hearts of the legionaries and auxiliaries who came tramping along this lonely road. It has the same effect nowadays on Pennine Way walkers.

Lambley Fell Colliery to the west of the village was an outlier of the great northern coalfield which runs through Durham and Northumberland; the sealed-off shaft is near the road where the Way reaches it. It was served by a special railway branch line which joined at Lambley with that from Haltwistle to Alston. Both colliery and railway are now, however, things of the past.

Despite two or three strategically placed signposts, the Way is not easy to follow beyond Lambley, although it starts off confidently enough. But eventually the footbridge over the Hartley Burn should be located which will lead on to the large farm of Batey Shield.

North of the farm the final obstacle of the day is a 2-mile (3 km) stretch of low-lying moorland; no difficulty should be found in the actual walking, but it is wise to check the direction of travel before starting up the moor. The dog-leg on the far side just above Gap Shield Farm is the most westerly point reached on the Pennine Way. After that there is only the A69 and a few fields alongside a golf course before the end of the walking at the Gilsland-Greenhead road, roughly where Hadrian's Wall crosses it.

Those expecting to find the Wall in all its glory, with milecastles and turrets, will be disappointed, however. There is a small scrap not far away, but it is not worth seeking. Far better to turn right, down into Greenhead, for the night's accommodation, and leave the glory of the Wall for the morrow.

The South Tyne near Slaggyford

DAY 15

HADRIAN'S WALL:
Greenhead to Twice Brewed

STARTING POINT
Greenhead (86-660654)
FINISHING POINT
Twice Brewed (86/87-753669)
LENGTH
7 miles (11 km)
ASCENT
1100 ft (340 m)
TERRAIN
A superb walk along the low ridge of
the Whin Sill following the line of the
Wall, but with many shallow but
steep sided valleys to be crossed.
Rather harder than it might appear.
REFRESHEMENTS
None along the way. Hotel/public
house at Twice Brewed.
ACCOMMODATION
Youth Hostel, hotel/public house and
guest houses at Twice Brewed slightly
off-route.

'I was tempted greatly here to trace the famous Picts Wall, built by the Romans, or rather rebuilt by them, from hence to Carlisle ... and I did go to several places in the fields thro' which it passed, where I saw the remains of it, some almost lost, some plain to be seen.'

Daniel Defoe, *A Tour through the Whole Island of Great Britain,*
1724–6

From Greenhead to Once Brewed, the Way follows the magnificent centre section of Hadrian's Wall—39–46 Roman miles (36–42 miles/58–68 km) along its 74-mile (119 km) length from its beginning at South Shields—as it runs along the crest of the great Whin Sill. Eight miles (13 km) at the most, including the final descent to the B6318 for overnight accommodation, the route is little more than an early morning stroll, on this, the shortest and easiest day of the journey! Some walkers may consider that Bellingham would be a better finishing point.

Such notions should be rejected out of hand. The way is considerably harder than distance alone would indicate, for a whole succession of steep-sided gaps, which break into the line of the crest, have to be negotiated during the day's walking. In any case, the wall is magnificent, the finest of all Roman remains in Britain and by far the most interesting feature met with along the Way. Well worth spending a day over! Apart from that 'small scrap' by the side of the Greenhead—Gilsland road—the Wall itself will not be seen until beyond Walltown Quarry, although the ditch is obvious as you come down from the golf course and stride up the hill beyond Thirlwall Castle. Actually a fortified residence, the castle was built about 1346 on a spur overlooking the River Tipalt, largely from stones looted from the Wall. It was one of several fortifications built in the English and Scottish Marches between the early-fourteenth and late-sixteenth centuries during the war with Scotland, when the need to protect lives and property became pressing. In its day it

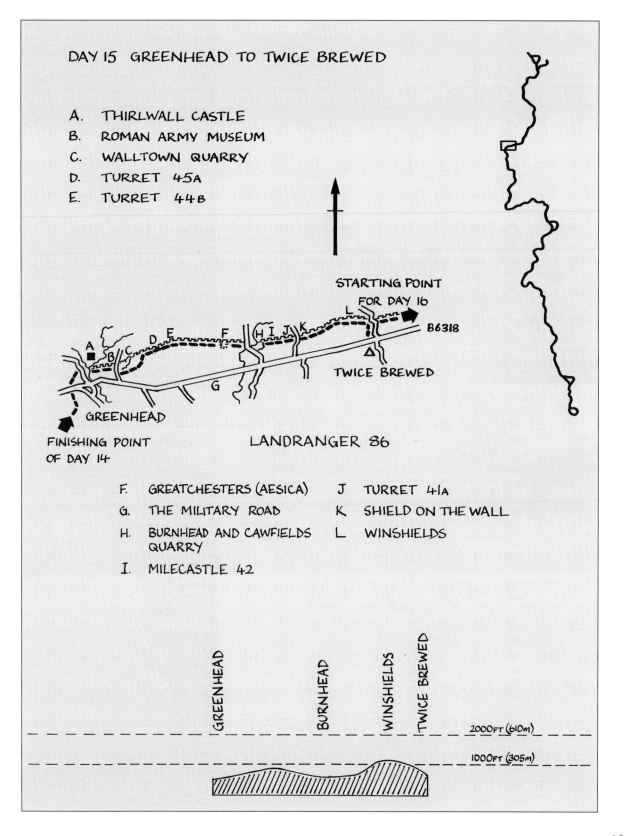

DAY 15 GREENHEAD TO TWICE BREWED

A. THIRLWALL CASTLE
B. ROMAN ARMY MUSEUM
C. WALLTOWN QUARRY
D. TURRET 45A
E. TURRET 44B

STARTING POINT FOR DAY 16

B6318

TWICE BREWED

GREENHEAD

FINISHING POINT OF DAY 14

LANDRANGER 86

F. GREATCHESTERS (AESICA)
G. THE MILITARY ROAD
H. BURNHEAD AND CAWFIELDS QUARRY
I. MILECASTLE 42
J. TURRET 41A
K. SHIELD ON THE WALL
L. WINSHIELDS

GREENHEAD BURNHEAD WINSHIELDS TWICE BREWED

2000FT (610M)

1000FT (305M)

was a substantial tower of four floors with an L-shaped cross-section; nowadays, it is an empty ruined shell of a building which nature is slowly reclaiming.

Whinstone (dolerite of the Whin Sill) was extracted in Walltown Quarry for about a hundred years until 1978. This not only removed a section of the Wall, but left a hole up to 100 ft (30 m) deep over an area of 40 acres (16 hectares), flooded in parts and with derelict buildings. Fortunately, Northumberland County Council purchased the site and, with a grant from the Department of the Environment, is now busily turning the area into an historical and archaeological theme park, which should be an improvement on what went before. But the lost section of the Wall has—alas!—gone for ever.

Walkers who have not been here before and who are by now impatient to view their first piece of genuine Roman Wall will not have long to wait. Five minutes or so is sufficient to take them to a superb section—one of the best—which runs along the top of the ridge from the far end of the quarry. A short distance to the right is their first turret, Number 45A. The numbering system for the Wall was the work of Professor R. G. Collingwood: the milecastles are numbered from 0 to 80 along the Wall from east to west, the two turrets between each pair taking the number of the milecastle to the east and suffixed either A or B. Thus, Turret 45A was the first turret after Milecastle 45 (no longer there) which was 45 Roman miles (41 miles/66 km) from the eastern end of the Wall. Originally built as a free-standing watchtower, it was incorporated into the Wall when that was constructed at a later date.

Just beyond the turret the Wall has again been destroyed by quarrying, but it resumes further along where it begins a steep descent into a small valley which breaks across the ridge. This small valley is Walltown Nick, the so-called Third Nick of Thirlwall. There were originally Nine Nicks of Thirlwall, but quarrying has removed all but five of them. Numbers Two and One (in that order) lie ahead. At each of the nicks a ditch was dug in front of the Wall for added strength; an unnecessary construction where the Wall was guarded by high cliffs.

About one mile (1.6 km) beyond the Third Nick is the fort of Aesica (Greatchesters). This was one of the great infantry forts which guarded the centre section of the Wall. There are a few things to be seen here, in particular the arch of the underground strongroom of the headquarters building, but most is grass-covered and awaits an expert hand to restore and consolidate it.

Cawfields Quarry beyond Greatchesters also destroyed an

Thirlwall Castle

THE WALL

Spartianus, writing in the fourth century, states that Hadrian built a wall 'to separate the barbarians from the Romans', and as Hadrian was in Britain in AD 122 the construction presumably began about then. Three legions were employed in building the Wall, which was largely completed by AD 128. It remained in use, except for short periods, for about 270 years.

The Wall ran for 80 Roman miles (74 miles/119 km) from Wallsend on the Tyne estuary to Bowness on the Solway Firth. Its eastern flank was secured by a line of milefortlets and watchtowers extending down the coast for a further 40 Roman miles (37 miles/59 km), while the harbour defences of the Tyne held the eastern end. There were also several outpost forts to the north of the Wall and two legionary fortresses at York and Chester which could provide support in emergencies.

The Wall was of stone, 15 ft (4.5 m) high with a parapet adding a further 6 ft (1.8 m), and 8–10 ft (2.4–3 m) thick. Milecastles, which had gates opening to north and south, were spaced at intervals of one Roman mile (1620 yards/1481 m), with two towers between each pair. The main fighting strength was accommodated in seventeen forts built into the Wall. Some, particularly to the east, were cavalry forts, while the others were for infantry. Finally, ditches were dug on both sides: one to the north for defensive purposes, one to the south as a line to demarcate the military zone.

Estimates of the number of soldiers on the Wall vary considerably, but it could have been as high as 24,000. The Wall itself would not have been guarded by the legions, but by auxiliaries raised in other provinces or even outside the Empire.

The Wall was not simply a static defence line to be held at all costs. Its design enabled large numbers of cavalry and infantry to be deployed rapidly in front of it. Given the superb fighting qualities of the Roman army, the combination of defence and aggression was highly efficient in dealing with any attack.

Militarily, the Wall was very successful. It was certainly breached at least twice, in AD 196–197 and 296, but only after its garrisons had been so reduced that it could no longer function as intended. It is true also that it was abandoned on two other occasions, but only because another wall, to the north, had made its use unnecessary. Economically, as an essential component of the Roman occupation of Britain, it was probably a failure owing to the enormous drain on revenues caused by such a large garrison.

Hadrian's Wall looking eastwards from Cuddy's Crags

appreciable section of the Wall, and Northumberland County Council should again be praised for the superb job of landscaping there.

The first extant milecastle met on this section (the much photographed Number 42) is at the top of a short rise out of the quarry. Milecastles held between twenty-five and fifty men each, housed in one or two barracks, and contained gateways to both north and south.

This one was built by the II Legion Augusta. From the hillside beyond there is an excellent view of the vallum running approximately parallel to the Wall down and over to the right. The farm nearby is named 'Shield on the Wall'; the word 'shield'—not uncommon around these parts—marking the locality of a 'shiel' to which cattle were taken for the summer in early-medieval times.

The final stretch of the day along the Wall is a long rise, broken by further dips, to its highest point at Winshields (1230 ft/375 m). The Wall appears and disappears; the presence of regular layers of dressed facingstone distinguishing it from lengths of conventional drystone walling. From the Ordnance Survey obelisk there is a superb view ahead over the Whin Sill and the loughs which lie to the north. It is an ideal place for a final rest.

A short distance further along, the Wall is left for Once Brewed Youth Hostel—or other accommodation—on the B6318 slightly further south. The journey up the Pennines is now almost at an end; tomorrow the Cheviots begin.

Hadrian's Wall, Winshields

DAY 16

THE BORDER FORESTS:
Twice Brewed to Bellingham

STARTING POINT
Twice Brewed (86/87-753669)
FINISHING POINT
Bellingham (80-840833)
LENGTH
16 miles (26 km)
ASCENT
1400 ft (430 m)
TERRAIN
Semi-moorland followed by some forest walking, finally across fields. Generally fairly easy walking.
REFRESHMENTS
None along the way. Hotel/public houses, café and shops in Bellingham.
ACCOMMODATION
A Youth Hostel, hotel/public houses and guest houses in Bellingham.

'Britanniam petiit, in qua multa correxit muramque per octoginta milia passuum primus duxit, qui barbaros Romanosque divideret.'

Spartianus, Fourth century

So numerous are the Roman remains in the area of the Wall that the unwary may be tempted to include the B6318, which runs in a long straight line just to the south. This, however, was a product of the eighteenth century and of the discovery during the invasion of England by the Jacobite army under Bonnie Prince Charlie that trans-Pennine communications were not all that they should be; so bad were they, in fact, that an English force, which was stationed at Newcastle, could not close with the enemy coming down the western flank. Built between 1751 and 1757, it is known to this day as 'the Military Road'. Unfortunately the Hanoverian engineers were none too particular where they got their materials or what they destroyed and large sections of the Wall were demolished as a result.

The presence of a Youth Hostel, a large inn which offers accommodation, numerous guesthouses and an Information Centre in this middle section of the Wall testify to its enormous popularity. The hostel—appropriately called Once Brewed to distinguish it from the inn, which is Twice Brewed—is large (only Edale, Haworth and Malham are larger) and modern (small bedrooms, cafeteria meal-service and flexible meal times).

Walkers forced to leave the Wall on the previous night to seek accommodation, will be overjoyed to discover this morning that the Pennine Way returns to the Wall for a further 2 miles (3 km), before leaving it for the north. This section is, moreover, by far the most picturesque encountered so far, for it runs along the top of the Whin Sill and offers superb views over a series of small lakes (called loughs—pronounced 'loffs'), relics of the great melt-down which took place at the end of the Ice Age. It is also—thanks to the National Trust—one of the few sections

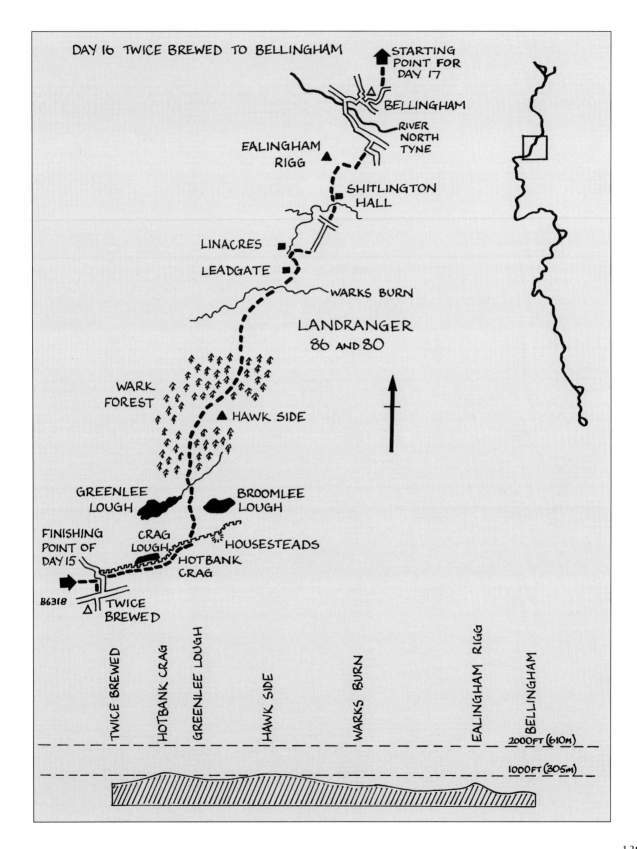

Above: Housesteads

where visitors are allowed to use the top of the Wall. Determined walkers will also push on as far as Housesteads —one of the great infantry forts of the centre section and the finest on the whole Wall because of extensive excavation and restoration—which lies about ¾ mile (1.2 km) further along from the Gap. But with a long day of 14 miles (23 km) ahead, a wary eye should be kept on the time.

From the Wall the Pennine Way heads directly northwards towards the great coniferous forests which can be seen ahead, crossing a fairly flat area of uninspired moor. Occasional backward glances will reveal the Whin Sill in all its glory; a scene that has changed little in the 1500 years since the Romans left. However hard Kirk Yetholm calls—and it should be calling loudly and clearly by this time—a little of your heart will be left behind on the Wall.

The Border Forests, which are centred on the enormous reservoir of Kielder Water, form the largest man-made forest in Western Europe, approximately 20–25 miles (32–40 km) across.

Opposite: Hadrian's Wall, Cuddy's Crags

Almost all of it belongs to the Forestry Commisssion, with only a small part owned by private forestry groups. In recent years the Commission has opened up its forests increasingly to the public and a substantial area has been designated as a Border Forest Park. Access is freely allowed in the Park, subject only to the need to carry out essential forestry operations and to sensible behaviour by visitors.

The Pennine Way—very wisely—avoids the main forest area by a great curving course around its eastern perimeter; two relatively small sections are caught, however: part of the Wark Forest at the south-east corner (Day 16) and part of Redesdale Forest at the north-east (Days 17 and 18). Forest walking is not to everybody's taste—some walkers find it highly enjoyable, others depressing; some lament the beauty lost, others comment that it is probably a lot better than what went before. One thing is certain: the forest roads enable you to build up a really good pace and catch up, if necessary, on time lost.

The Wark Forest section is broken at about its mid-point by a bare stretch of moorland, bordered on three sides by the forest and on the fourth by the long edge of Hawk Side Hill (this name is not just another sad reflection on what once was and is now no more, for sparrow-hawks have increased considerably in numbers with the growth of the forests). Along the way there is a lovely drystone-walled enclosure with a few declining trees and short-cropped turf that makes an ideal spot for a late morning break.

The Way finally emerges from the forest near the Forestry Commission settlement of Stonehaugh, which was established in 1950, although nothing will be seen of it. A mile (1.6 km) further along it crosses the Warks Burn over a small footbridge. The Burn is one of the many small gems along the Way that tend to go unnoticed amid the greater splendours. Yet it is a delightful place of dark pools, small shaley cliffs, shingle reaches and mossy, primrose-covered banks. The haunt of dipper and of wagtail. Worth an hour of anybody's time. Ah! If only it could be spared!

Beyond the burn the way is over pastures and meadows; gentle country with farm following farm. Horneystead then Leadgate, Lowstead then Linacres, Brownsleazes then Shitlington. Only the final obstacle of Ealingham Rigg with its steep craggy front—surmounted by going up a slanting groove—now stands between the walker and Bellingham.

Bellingham (pronounced 'Bellingjum') is the last town before the end at Kirk Yetholm, although some provisions can be picked up at Byrness. It is probably best to arrive early and catch the shops.

Above: The Warks Burn

Opposite: Footbridge over the Warks Burn

DAY 17

APPROACHING THE BORDER:

Bellingham to Byrness

STARTING POINT
Bellingham (80-840833)
FINISHING POINT
Byrness (80-765027)
LENGTH
15 miles (24 km)
ASCENT
1550 ft (470 m)
TERRAIN
Rolling moorland followed by a long
forest stretch.
REFRESHMENTS
None along the way. Hotel/public
house, café and shops at Byrness.
ACCOMMODATION
A Youth Hostel, hotel/public house
and guest houses at Byrness.

'And he has burn'd the dales of Tyne,
and part of Bambrough shire;
And three good towers on Roxburgh fells,
He left them all on fire.'

'The Battle of Otterbourne' (Anon)

From the ninth century, when Kenneth Mac Alpin claimed all
the lands from the Forth to the Tweed, until the unification of
the Scottish and English crowns in 1603, the border area was a
disputed place. A factor in this was the system of inheri-
tance—called 'gavelkind'—under which possessions were
divided equally between sons. As individual holdings became
smaller and gradually lost their viability, families were forced to
look elsewhere to make ends meet, and the stealing of
livestock—and anything worth having—became a fact of life.
In any case the high, rounded hill country of the Cheviots did

Padon Hill

144

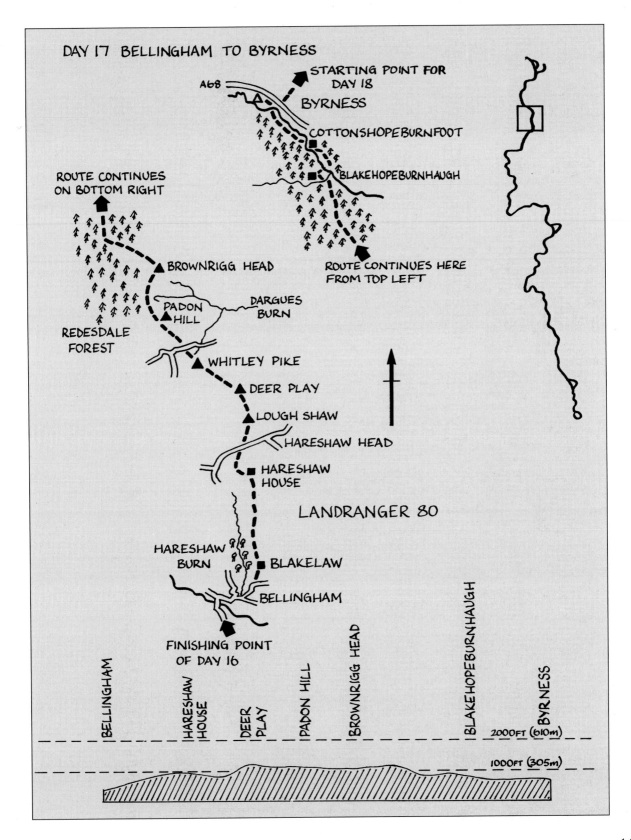

DAY 17 BELLINGHAM TO BYRNESS

A68

STARTING POINT FOR DAY 18

BYRNESS

COTTONSHOPEBURNFOOT

BLAKEHOPEBURNHAUGH

ROUTE CONTINUES ON BOTTOM RIGHT

ROUTE CONTINUES HERE FROM TOP LEFT

BROWNRIGG HEAD

PADON HILL

DARGUES BURN

REDESDALE FOREST

WHITLEY PIKE

DEER PLAY

LOUGH SHAW

HARESHAW HEAD

HARESHAW HOUSE

LANDRANGER 80

HARESHAW BURN

BLAKELAW

BELLINGHAM

FINISHING POINT OF DAY 16

BELLINGHAM

HARESHAW HOUSE

DEER PLAY

PADON HILL

BROWNRIGG HEAD

BLAKEHOPEBURNHAUGH

BYRNESS

2000FT (610m)

1000FT (305m)

145

not make it easy to draw accurate boundary lines and this in itself led inevitably to constant disagreements. As if that was not bad enough, the opening of a campaign against the Scots by Edward I in 1296 ushered in some three centuries of warfare in which Northumberland featured prominently. All in all, life on the border was hard, insecure and dangerous.

The emptiness of the Border lands, in which there are few large villages or towns, can certainly be attributed to those centuries of constant conflict, although later events—such as the breaking up of monastery holdings and the eviction of communities to enable greedy landowners to form estates or to change over to extensive sheep farming—played their part. Deserted villages are common in Northumberland, and no other county had a greater number of castles and other fortified structures.

In the journey of the Pennine Way from Hadrian's Wall to the end at Kirk Yetholm, 59 miles (95 km) over four days, only two communities are met and only one, Bellingham, is of any size. The going over that part of the Way is not tough in the sense that the going from Edale to Crowden in Longdendale is tough, but the miles are the loneliest miles of all.

From Bellingham an ideal route for the Way would have been up the valley of the Hareshaw Burn, which runs roughly northwards from its confluence with the North Tyne. That way would have taken the walker through beautiful ancient woodlands to the magnificent waterfall of Hareshaw Linn. Instead, however, the Way takes a parallel course across low moorlands to the east of the valley until the road to Otterburn is crossed near Hareshaw Head.

In mid-Victorian times a large ironworks was in operation at Bellingham, supplied with fuel from a colliery at Hareshaw Head. Some spoil heaps can be seen on both sides of the road where the Way crosses it. The ironworks supplied a good-quality product, some of which found its way into George Stephenson's High Level Bridge situated not too far away at Newcastle.

From the Otterburn road the Pennine Way starts a long moorland crossing of about 5 miles (8 km), over or near a series of minor tops—Deer Play, Whitley Pike, Padon Hill and Brownrigg Head. On a good day, this is a pleasant walk, although without any particular distinction. The monument on Padon Hill is a good landmark, first seen long before you pass it. However, most attention will probably centre on the dark line of conifers ahead which marks the beginning of Redesdale Forest. The Way dallies around it for a while, but finally plunges in a short distance beyond Brownrigg Head.

Hareshaw Linn – a worthwhile diversion from the route

Redesdale Forest is the most northerly of those which make up the Border Forest Park. This forest section continues all the way to Byrness, and is far longer than that already encountered further south. In some parts clearance is revealing a landscape that has not been seen for many years, for tree growth will gradually obscure all but the most prominent features. But, most of the way, the tall dark-green walls of densely packed conifers hug closely about the path, so that progress is measured only by the passage of the numerous forest roads or by a growing weariness in spirit and limb.

The small group of buildings at Blakehopeburnhaugh (the longest place-name of the Way so far) marks the arrival into the valley of the Rede. 'Haughs' (pronounced 'hoffs') were small areas of relatively flat land by rivers or streams, much prized for cultivation; this word is common, therefore, in Northumbrian place-names. The Way continues in the forest, however, past Cottonshopeburnfoot (now the longest place-name of the Way to date!), generally following the river until Byrness is reached.

Byrness is a Forestry Commission village built in the early 1950s for workers in the great forests. With developments in mechanization, however, fewer workers than was envisaged are now needed and it is only about one third of its intended size. It is a slightly utilitarian-looking place, but Pennine Way walkers will find comforts enough. A Youth Hostel occupies two of a row of cottages, there is a store and a post office (for those last cards home!) and, down the road, a café and a hotel. There is nothing more or better between here and Kirk Yetholm except two small mountain huts and the occasional farm well away from the line of your journey.

Byrness Church

DAY 18

THE CHEVIOT HILLS:
Byrness to Clennell Street

STARTING POINT
Byrness (80-765027)
FINISHING POINT
Crossing point with Clennell Street
(80-872161)
LENGTH
14 miles (22 km)
ASCENT
2600 ft (800 m)
TERRAIN
A steep climb followed by the
traverse of the main ridge over a
series of tops. Follows the Border
Fence for much of the way.
REFRESHMENTS
None along the way.
ACCOMMODATION
A descent may be made from the
ridge at the end of the day to farms
which offer accommodation, although
this will add several miles to the
journey (advance booking is advised).
MOUNTAIN REFUGE HUT
A small wooden hut on the line of the
Way situated at Yearning Saddle (80-
804129).

'. . . I think probably that I would plump for the Cheviots as my
favourite ground . . .'

Tom Stephenson, 1965

Walkers on the Pennine Way divide into two groups at Byrness:
those who intend to reach Kirk Yetholm in one day and those
who do not. That decision determines their time of departure;
for the former 6 or 7 am is not too early, for the latter 9 am is
not too late. If time permits, two days for the final stretch is to
be preferred; in bad weather the full distance may prove too
severe, in good weather the attractions of the ridge demand a
more leisurely approach. In case of emergency there are two
mountain huts situated at strategic points along the ridge; the
first just before Lamb Hill, the second much further along
between Auchope Cairn and The Schil.

The steepest climb of the day—a direct line to the summit of
Byrness Hill—must be faced right at the beginning. It is best to
grit your teeth and face it resolutely, secure in the knowledge
that there is nothing worse to come. A while ago this hill was
crowned by a small fire tower, but now only the concrete base
remains.

From the summit the Way heads almost due north for about 3
miles (5 km), slowly gaining height and keeping just outside the
edge of Redesdale Forest along the crest of a broad ridge.
Prominent notices over the right mark the limit of the
Otterburn Training Area—the largest in Britain—used for live
firing as well as troop manoeuvres. Almost unbelievably, this
covers a total area of 92 square miles (23, 828 hectares), 20% of
the National Park. Its presence here is a disgrace.

The Scotland-England border runs along the northern end of
the forest and just before Chew Green the Way crosses it briefly
for no very obvious reason. Although the border will be
followed closely now until Black Hag, at the beginning of the
final descent into the valley of the Halter Burn, the Way

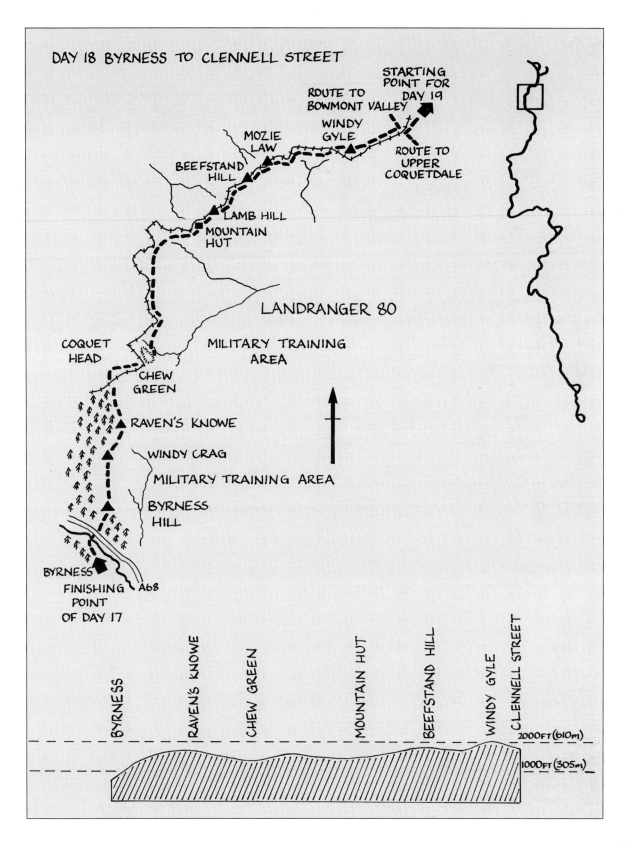

DAY 18 BYRNESS TO CLENNELL STREET

STARTING POINT FOR DAY 19

ROUTE TO BOWMONT VALLEY

WINDY GYLE

MOZIE LAW

ROUTE TO UPPER COQUETDALE

BEEFSTAND HILL

LAMB HILL

MOUNTAIN HUT

LANDRANGER 80

COQUET HEAD

MILITARY TRAINING AREA

CHEW GREEN

RAVEN'S KNOWE

WINDY CRAG

MILITARY TRAINING AREA

BYRNESS HILL

BYRNESS

FINISHING POINT OF DAY 17

A68

BYRNESS

RAVEN'S KNOWE

CHEW GREEN

MOUNTAIN HUT

BEEFSTAND HILL

WINDY GYLE

CLENNELL STREET

2000FT (610m)

1000FT (305m)

stays—with the exception of one short stretch—firmly on the English side.

For a time in AD 80 the area around Chew Green was a hive of activity, for it was a stopping point for the Ninth Legion during Agricola's campaign into southern Scotland. The earthworks of the Marching Camp which they constructed can still be seen across a green spur in the valley to the right of the main ridge. Later a supply road, Dere Street, was laid down along the line of march from Corbridge on the Wall to Inveresk on the Firth of Forth, and a small permanent fort was established here to protect convoys which came along it. Obligingly, the Way drops down towards the site to skirt the complex of earthworks on their southern and eastern sides, but closeness destroys appreciation and the best views of them are from the hillsides.

From the camp the Way follows Dere Street for a mile (1.6 km) or so until the Border Fence—which runs along the entire length of the border over the Cheviots—is reached. From this point until the end of the day's walking the Way follows the fence, keeping more or less on the top of the main ridge. Over one stretch an official short-cut is made to shorten the way around an obvious corner and in other places canny walkers have added their own, but otherwise the fence is an infallible guide, and map and compass can be safely put away. The going varies from poor to good; in particular, the section around Lamb Hill and Beefstand Hill has seen better days.

At the meeting point with the Border Fence the real Cheviot walking begins. Nothing that you have encountered before quite equals the splendour of the final walk along the great ridge. How sound was Tom Stephenson's judgment on the Cheviot Hills and how fortunate his decision to continue the Pennine Way over them, rather than give it its ending on the Wall! At only one point on this day does the height exceed 2000 ft (610 m), but nobody who walks this way will doubt for one moment that this is real mountain country. Always there is the ridge ahead and always wonderful, rolling, grassy hills and deep, winding, intriguing valleys on either hand. A succession of tops—Lamb Hill, Beefstand Hil and Mozie Law—offer superb all-round views, with Windy Gyle, towards the end of the day, providing the finest of them all.

In the days of border conflict, this section—from Hanging Stone near the Cheviot summit to Kershopefoot in Liddesdale—was the worst. Armed bands—mosstroopers or reivers—came this way from Scotland into England, choosing quiet ways through the hills so that their attack would be the more effective. The Wardens of the March—usually one of the

Above: The view from Windy Gyle

Opposite: The ascent of Byrness Hill

leading border lords made responsible by royal appointment for border security—did their best to maintain the peace by the posting of sentries at strategic points, but these were not particularly effective; there were always more crossing points than sentries and sufficient opportunities to ensure a worthwhile return. Crossing points on the border were also used as meeting places for lords from both sides where, hopefully, grievances could be aired and wrongs put right.

Some of the ways across the ridge—which are still well defined—were important drove roads or packhorse trails. The Street, along which the Way runs for a short distance near Mozie Law, was a drove road from Hownam to the north of the ridge into Upper Coquetdale to the south; Clennell Street, which crosses near Windy Gyle, was another drove road from Mowhaugh to Alwinton; and Salter's Road was a packhorse trail which carried salt from the brine pits on Tyneside over the border into Scotland.

The summit of Windy Gyle possesses the largest cairn on the Pennine Way, Russell's Cairn, named after Lord Francis Russell, who was killed here in 1585. There is also a memorial cairn, a wall shelter, an Ordnance Survey obelisk, and one of those curious metal stars which decorate the Border Fence in this area. The view is breathtaking and the finest until The Schil is reached late on the final day.

About one mile (1.6 km) beyond Windy Gyle the main ridge of the Cheviots can be left along a convenient crossing path for a descent into Upper Coquetdale (to the south) or the Bowmont valley (to the north). Either way involves a descent of at least 1½–2 miles (1.8–3.2 km) before any accommodation is encountered, which has to be made good next morning. Most walkers, however, will regard those options as infinitely preferable to struggling on for the remainder of the way to Kirk Yetholm, particularly if the Cheviot itself is to be climbed. Alternatives, of course, are a bivouac or a camp on or just off the ridge.

Russell's Cairn

DAY 19

THE FINAL STAGE:
Kirk Yetholm

STARTING POINT
Crossing point with Clennell Street
(80-872161)
FINISHING POINT
Kirk Yetholm (74-827282)
LENGTH
14 miles (22 km)
ASCENT
2300 ft (700 m)
TERRAIN
Continues along the Border Fence
with a diversion to the summit of The
Cheviot. The final miles are either
along a road in the valley of the
Halter Burn, or a continuation of the
ridge until a descent can be made into
the valley much further along.
REFRESHMENTS
None along the way.
ACCOMMODATION
A Youth Hostel, hotel/public house
and guest houses at Kirk Yetholm and
nearby Town Yetholm.
MOUNTAIN REFUGE HUT
A small wooden hut on the way
between Auchope Cairn and The
Schil (74-880201).

'The Pennine Way is King!'

Walker on arriving at Kirk Yetholm, 1974

After eighteen days of continuous walking, from that first
exciting mile up Grindsbrook Clough at Edale, it will be difficult
to believe that the great adventure is now almost at an end—for
an adventure it has been, every step of the way. But only 13½
miles (21.5 km) now remain before Kirk Yetholm. Ideally the
sun will be shining out of a cloudless blue sky, and everything
will be wonderfully green and fresh and sparkling, and you will
be fit and tanned and raring to go. A short climb to the main
ridge and the real walking of the day begins!

From the crossing path between Upper Coquetdale and the
Bowmont valley the Way continues along the Border Fence
which goes in a great S-shape, stretched out over some 3 miles
(5 km) or so, an easy walk which slowly gains height as it goes
along. There are good views back towards Windy Gyle and

The end of the Way: The green at Kirk
Yetholm

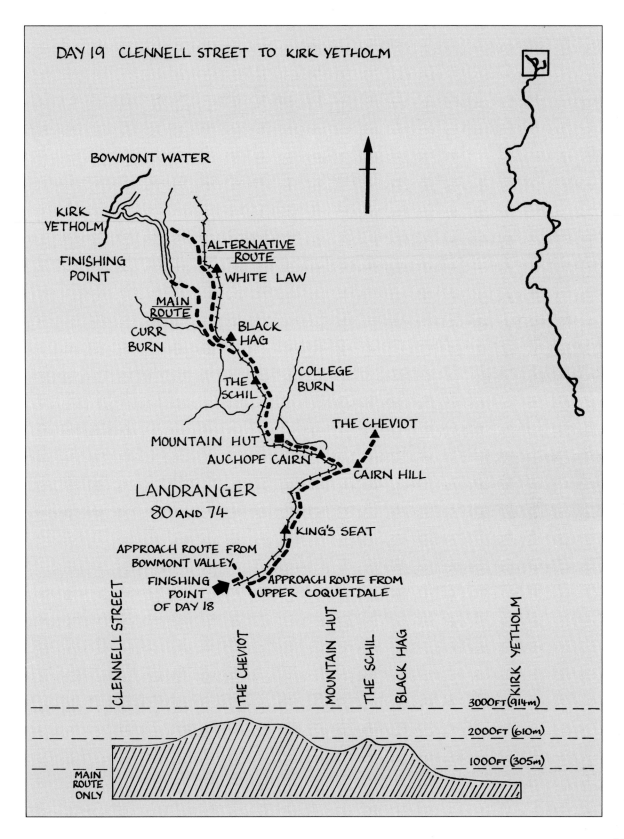

DAY 19 CLENNELL STREET TO KIRK YETHOLM

BOWMONT WATER

KIRK YETHOLM

FINISHING POINT

ALTERNATIVE ROUTE

WHITE LAW

MAIN ROUTE

CURR BURN

BLACK HAG

COLLEGE BURN

THE SCHIL

THE CHEVIOT

MOUNTAIN HUT

AUCHOPE CAIRN

CAIRN HILL

LANDRANGER 80 AND 74

KING'S SEAT

APPROACH ROUTE FROM BOWMONT VALLEY

FINISHING POINT OF DAY 18

APPROACH ROUTE FROM UPPER COQUETDALE

CLENNELL STREET

THE CHEVIOT

MOUNTAIN HUT

THE SCHIL

BLACK HAG

KIRK YETHOLM

3000FT (914m)

2000FT (610m)

1000FT (305m)

MAIN ROUTE ONLY

157

forward towards the Cheviot, but as usual it is those away from the main ridge which are the best. Extensive forests can be seen in both directions, but lack the dominating presence that they have further south, while in one or two places a happy coincidence of flanking hills permits the briefest glimpse of a distant farmstead, Uswayford or Sourhope. But otherwise, there is little, only the glorious, rolling Cheviots themselves.

At an unnamed top, a short distance before Auchope Cairn, the Border Fence makes an abrupt change of direction. At this point a major decision has to be taken: to include the Cheviot or not? Technically, it is part of the Pennine Way and should be included, but it is over a mile (1.6 km) there and the same back again. What is more, it is a hard mile—a very hard mile—of endless, energy-sapping, glutinous peat bogs, without even the consolation of a decent view at the end of it. Without doubt, this is the point on the Pennine Way where your cards are called. If you have the time and the energy, do it!—or you may spend the rest of your life regretting that you 'chickened out' when the going got really tough.

Back on the Border Fence a short walk westwards leads to Auchope Cairn. The impressive ravine over to the right is Hen Hole, in the upper reaches of the College Burn; an impressive place of black, columnar cliffs and rivulets of reddish scree. In the distance—half-right from the Cairn—is the Schil, the last summit on the Way.

There is a great loss of height between Auchope Cairn and the Schil, but a feeling that the end is now near is unmistakable and most will tackle it with enthusiasm. The second mountain hut is located at a low point between the two. This was erected in 1988 and dedicated to the memory of Stuart Lancaster. The shelter is there for the use of all who come this way, the only condition being that they '. . . keep it in a clean and tidy condition for those that follow'.

Frank Smythe, a noted 'Everester' of the interwar years, shrewdly observed that height itself was of little account in assessing the worth of any mountain. Nowhere is this better illustrated than with the Schil. Failing by a small amount to reach the magic figure of 2000 ft (610 m), which is usually regarded in Britain as the minimum altitude for a mountain, it has more character about it than many far higher peaks. It is also the finest view-point on the Pennine Way. Well worth coming over 255 miles (410 km) to visit, it makes a fitting end to the walk over the Cheviot Hills.

On the col between The Schil and the next top, Black Hag,

The Border Fence near The Schil

the Way crosses the Border Fence for the last time and heads into Scotland. From this point two ways may be chosen for the final miles to the finish at Kirk Yetholm.

The first—and the recommended one if the weather is favourable—continues northwards along the ridge for a further 2½ miles (4 km) over White Law before dropping down into the valley of the Halter Burn. The alternative route in contrast immediately seeks the lower ground, initially in a rather misleading move towards the adjacent valley of the Curr Burn—it is not unknown for walkers to arrive in Kirk Yetholm from the wrong direction—until its true intention is revealed with a sweep to the north.

Either way, once the valley of the Halter Burn is reached, the rest is all straight-forward, along a quiet country lane until the village green at Kirk Yetholm is reached. It should—if your day has gone well—be late afternoon or early evening when you arrive at the end of your journey.

A view from the Schil

GENERAL INFORMATION ABOUT THE WAY

Official Opening
24 April 1965 by the Right Hon. F.T. Willey, Minister of Land and Natural Resources, near Malham Tarn before about 2000 people. Other speakers were Lord Strang, Chairman of the National Parks Commission, and Tom Stephenson

Starting point
Grindsbrook Booth, Edale, Derbyshire (110-123860).
Finishing point
Kirk Yetholm, Borders, Scotland (74-827282).
The most westerly point reached
Gap Shields Fan (86-641643) just south of Hadrian's Wall.
The most easterly point reached
The starting point at Edale (110-123860).
Length
The nominal length is 250 miles (402 km), but some guide books give slightly greater distances. Wainwright in *Pennine Way Companion* gives 270 miles (435 km), but this is on a different basis which attempts to assess the 'miles of walking . . . taking into account the contours and the nature of the ground . . .' An assessment for this book gave 261 miles (420 km) for the main route, but the distance actually walked will certainly be greater.
Amount of ascent
Impossible to estimate accurately, but an assessment for this book using map contours suggests about 32,300 ft (9850 m). Owing to the roughness of the ground the true figure is certainly greater.
Counties crossed
Seven English counties (Derbyshire, Greater Manchester, West Yorkshire, North Yorkshire, Durham, Cumbria and Northumberland) and one Scottish county (Borders) are traversed.
Mountain summits traversed
It is usually considered that a mountain top in Britain is a height of 2000 ft (610 m) or more, but the term really needs closer definition than that. The main summits reached are:
Bleaklow Head 2077 ft (633 m) Peak District (110-092959)

Pen-y-ghent 2277 ft (694 m) Yorkshire Dales (98-839734)
Great Shunner Fell 2349 ft (716 m) Yorkshire Dales (98-849973)
Knock Fell 2605 ft (794 m) Northern Pennines (91-721302)
Great Dun Fell 2779 ft (847 m) Northern Pennines (91-710322)
Little Dun Fell 2762 ft (842 m) Northern Pennines (91-704330)
Cross Fell 2930 ft (893 m) Northern Pennines (91-687344)
Windy Gyle 2031 ft (619 m) Cheviot Hills (80-856152)
The Cheviot 2674 ft (815 m) Cheviot Hills (74-909205)
In each case the metric figure is the definitive figure and the imperial figure calculated from it.
Surveys
Three detailed surveys on the number and type of walkers on the Way have been carried out: (1) *Pennine Way: Survey of Use,* National Parks Commission, 1965; (2) *Pennine Way Survey,* Countryside Commission, 1971; (3) *Study of walkers on the Pennine Way,* English Tourist Board, 1979. Of these, the 1971 survey was by far the most comprehensive.

How many complete the Way each year?
Nobody seems to know! The three surveys given above were all carried out in the peak walking period of July-September (apart from one pilot survey at Easter 1971) and therefore give no information on the remainder of the year, a period of over nine months. For that reason none gives any assessment for the total number who complete the Way. However, using this data and that obtained from surveys on other long distance paths and making various reasonable assumptions, it is possible to make an assessment. This suggests that around 1979 (the time of the last survey) about 2250 walkers were completing the Pennine Way each year.
Is the use increasing?
Yes, it appears so. On the evidence available it

seems that there was a three-fold increase between 1965 and 1971 and a two-fold increase between 1971 and 1979.

Distance walked and duration of stay

In the 1971 survey about two thirds of those interviewed were long-distance walkers spending one night or more along the Way. Of these nearly half walked the entire distance, the remainder walking just part of the Way. Of those who walked the entire way, 63% took between sixteen and twenty-two days, 31% took fifteen days or less, and 6% took more than twenty-two days. The average time to complete the Way was nineteen days.

Which way do they go?

Both the 1971 and 1979 surveys showed that the vast majority of walkers, and particularly the long-distance walkers, travel from south to north. In 1979 76% of all walkers went northwards, ie 82% of long-distance walkers and 70% of day walkers did so. Probably the most important reason for this is that all guide books (with one exception) describe the route in that direction, but there is probably also a psychological factor.

What sort of people use the Way?

They are predominantly male: for example, in 1971 67% of all adult walkers were males. The greater the distance travelled the more likely this is to be true. As would be expected, most of them were adult, although children under fifteen made up a surprising 15% of all walkers in 1971 and an even more surprising 24% in 1979. But, not surprisingly, the adult walkers tend to be young people; in 1971 about half the adult long-distance walkers were below twenty-five and 86% below

forty-four. Day walkers on the whole tend to be older. Perhaps surprisingly, only about one in five long-distance walkers belonged to a walking club.

Where do the walkers come from?

In 1971 almost entirely from England, as Scotland and Wales could muster only 3% between them (it is suggested that this is because they have their own mountains!) while 2% came from abroad. The figures were broadly similar in 1979.

How well equipped are walkers on the Way?

It seems that long-distance walkers are reasonably well equipped, as almost all had boots, waterproof clothing, warm spare clothing, a compass, a map and a guide. A fair number, however, were not carrying a whistle, First Aid equipment or a reserve food ration, all of which are usually recommended for walks in wild country. As might be expected, the day walkers were less well equipped.

How large are the parties?

In 1971 64% of long-distance walkers were making the journey with family or friends in a party of two or three people. Only 27% were in an organized party (which would usually be much larger) and a mere 9% were walking alone.

What attracted walkers to the Way?

'The challenge' was the main reason given by long-distance walkers, with quality of scenery, peace and quiet and the uniqueness of the experience much less important. Natural history, historical and archaeological features, or simply the desire to visit a particular place, had remarkably little appeal. It seems that walking the Way is sufficient unto itself.

The Weather of the Pennines

At all times of the year the most frequent winds come from the west and south-west, but winds from almost any direction may be experienced. In any case, smooth air flow is unusual and eddies may produce rapid changes in both direction and speed. As might be expected, wind speeds increase with altitude; Great Dun Fell has an average of 100 days of gale each year (a day of gale is defined as one where the wind attains a mean speed of 34 knots (39 mph) or more over any period of ten minutes). Winds are normally stronger during the winter months and also during daytime.

On average the warmest part of the year is July–August and the coldest December–February, but the range of extreme temperatures which have been recorded in each month is very wide. It should also be remembered that temperature decreases with increasing altitude at the rate of 0.5°C for each 100 m (328 ft). Finally, wind will increase the rate at which the body loses heat, producing the same feeling of cold as would be experienced on a still day at a much lower air temperature. For example, a wind of 20 knots at an air temperature of 8°C will produce a similar effect to an air temperature of –25°C in still conditions. June has the most sunshine and December the least, but the amount decreases with increasing latitude and altitude.

Rainfall in the Pennines is greatly influenced both by locality and altitude. Generally speaking, as high ground forces air to rise with consequent cooling, the heaviest rainfall occurs on the higher ground and the lightest in lowland areas. As the prevailing winds which bring the rain come from the Atlantic to the west there is a pronounced rain-shadow effect from both the Pennines and the Lake District. Thus lowland areas to the east of the Pennines have a much lower average annual rainfall than those to the west. This is particularly noticeable in the Eden valley, which experiences very low rainfall owing to the protection of the Lake District mountains. Over the course of the year the period April–June tends to be driest (July–September is not so good) and the November–January period the wettest. It should be borne in mind that rainfall in summer is often for relatively short periods but intense, in contrast to winter rainfall, which is less intense but over a longer period. By comparison, therefore, the winter may seem wetter than the actual rainfall figures suggest.

These comments are based upon average performances, however, and conceal considerable differences between years. Kielder Castle, to the west of the Cheviots, for example, has an average

Eden Valley from Great Dun Fell

June rainfall of 73 mm; the actual figures vary from 33 to 154 mm. (The highest rainfall recorded in a single day in June is higher than that recorded for the whole of the driest month!)

As might be expected, snowfall increases as you go higher or further north. Over the highest ground of the Pennines falls may take place in almost any month, but snow cover is generally restricted to the period October–May. (Snow covered some parts of the Pennines on Coronation Day, 2 June 1953, and Cross Fell after an extremely bad winter was still covered on 10 July 1951.) January and February are usually the worst months for snowfall or snow cover, but December and March can be bad. On average, snow falls on the higher ground of the Pennines on seventy or more days each year. High snowfall in combination with strong winds can cause heavy drifting, particularly on higher ground.

Visibility is of great importance on the Pennine Way, partly because good views are lost if it is bad, but also because of difficulties in navigation. Radiation fogs, which fill valleys and cover lowland areas in a thick blanket, are largely a phenomenon of the winter months, when they form during the night or early morning. Although occasionally they will last all day, it is normal for them to clear away gradually. As the walker climbs out of the valley where he has spent the night, he will break through the fog layer into clear conditions. Fogs of this type are usually associated with clear skies, light winds and fairly damp conditions.

Mountains and high moorland—usually above about 1500 ft (460 m)—are often enveloped in low cloud, a phenomenon referred to as hill fog. Unlike radiation fogs these may be accompanied by winds, rain or snow. On the Way they are a far more serious problem than radiation fogs as they occur on uplands, which are usually more featureless and route finding can be difficult.

Generally speaking, fogs are least frequent in the June–August period and most frequent in December–February. Recordings over many years at Great Dun Fell show that visibility is less than 44 yard (40 m) on an average of fifty-five mornings and less than 210 yards (200 m) on an average of 239 mornings each year. This will be due entirely to hill fogs.

Pennine Terms

Batter	The inward lean of the faces of a drystone wall so that the top is narrower than the base
Bog	A marshy area on a peat moor
Buttress	A prominent face of rock standing out from a cliff or hillside
Cairn	A heap of stones marking a path or a mountain summit
Calf	Male and female cattle less than one year old
Clapper bridge	Small footbridge formed from one or more wide, flat slabs of rock
Clints	The top surface of limestone blocks in pavement areas
Clough	Steep-sided valleys cut into moorland slopes by streams (also cleugh)
Coping stones	Flat stones which are placed on edge along the top of a drystone wall (also known as top, capping and cap stones)
Cow	Female cattle which has had at least two calves
Cripple hole	A small square hole in a wall to allow passage to sheep (also creep or thirl hole)
Dale	A valley
Dyke	Drystone wall (also dike)

Edge	A long line of millstone grit crag along the edge of moorland	*Outbye*	Moorland grazing away from a farm
Enclosure	The enclosing of land by hedges or stone walls	*Pasture*	Improved land used for grazing but not for hay production
Ewe	Female sheep after first shearing or lamb	*Pavements*	A bare area of limestone (see clints, grykes, runnels)
Fell	An area of moorland	*Pot-hole*	(1) A vertical shaft, often wide and deep, formed in limestone areas by streams; (2) Round holes formed in the limestone beds of streams
Filling stones	Small stones placed into the central cavity of drystone walls (also hearting)		
Footings	Large stones used as the base of a drystone wall	*Ram*	Uncastrated male sheep (also tup)
Ginnel	A narrow pathway between walls or buildings	*Resurgence*	The place where an underground stream reappears above ground in limestone areas
Grough	Deep channel cut into peat moorland by water	*Runnels*	Shallow grooves formed on clints in pavement areas by the action of water draining from the blocks
Grykes	Deep vertical fissures in limestone pavements		
Hag	An isolated hummock with walls of bare peat	*Scree*	Small stones covering a hillside (also glidders)
Heifer	A cow between its first service and its second calf	*Shake hole*	A funnel-shaped depression in limestone areas caused by soil subsidence
Hogg	A young sheep which has not been sheared (a gimmer hogg is a female sheep)	*Shippon*	Barn which houses cattle in winter (also byre)
Inbye	Improved grassland around a farm	*Sink*	The place where a stream disappears underground in limestone areas (also sink hole, swallow hole, swallet or shack hole)
Lamb	Male or female sheep less than six months old		
Level	A mine tunnel cut from the bottom of a shaft or into a hillside	*Sough*	A long drainage tunnel in a lead mine
Lough	Lake	*Stirk*	Male or female cattle from one to two years old
Lynchets	Flat terraces cut into hillsides by farmers in medieval times	*Stones*	A small outcrop of gritstone
Masham	Sheep produced by crossing a Swaledale or Dalesbred ewe with a Teeswater or Wensleydale ram	*Store cattle*	Beef cattle raised on hill farms for sale to lowland farms, where they are fattened before slaughter
Meadow	Field carrying a hay crop	*Through stones*	Stones, usually flat, set through the full thickness of a drystone wall and often protruding on each side (also tie stones)
Millstone grit	A coarse, hard-wearing sandstone forming the summit cap of many mountains and moorland areas		
Mule	Sheep produced by crossing a Swaledale ewe with a Bluefaced Leicester ram (also greyface)	*Tor*	A hilltop; also refers to a weathered gritstone outcrop
		Wether	Castrated male sheep

ACCOMMODATION

The 1971 survey (see page 162) showed that 41% of all nights on the Way were spent in tents, 30% in Youth Hostels, 25% in bed and breakfast accommodation and 4% in other types, e.g., in barns or with friends. As the Youth Hostel chain has improved considerably since 1971, it is likely that the proportion of nights spent in them has risen. In practice, most walkers probably use a variety of types of accommodation, rather than relying entirely on any one.

Youth Hostels
The advantages of Hostels are: (a) they are considerably cheaper than other forms of accommodation except camping (b) most hostels offer a full service of bed, breakfast, evening meal and packed lunch packet, and cooking facilities (c) they are ideal for the inevitable period of bad weather as they always have good washing and drying facilities for clothes (d) they provide the opportunity to meet other walkers along the Way so that information and reminiscences can be exchanged—the sense of camaraderie that develops between fellow-travellers along the Way has to be experienced to be appreciated.

The disadvantages are: (a) most Hostels are closed for one day each week, even in summer (b) a high proportion close altogether for periods during the winter (c) there are gaps in the Youth Hostel chain.

In order from the south, the following Youth Hostels are situated on or near to the Way (position indicated by Landranger sheet number followed by grid reference). The notes refer to the Youth Hostels as numbered. Edale (110-139865) (1); Crowden (110-073993) (2); Mankinholes (103-960235) (3); Haworth (104-038378) (4); Earby (103-915468) (5); Malham (98-901629); Stainforth (98-821668) (6); Hawes (98-867897); Keld (92-891009); Baldersdale (92-931179); Langdon Beck (91-860304); Dufton (91-688251); Alston (86-717461); Greenhead (86-659655) (7); Once Brewed (86-752668); Bellingham (80-843834); Byrness (80-764027); Kirk Yetholm (74-

826282) (8).
Special features:
1 This hostel is situated about 2 miles (3 km) from the start of the Pennine Way at Edale. Hathersage YH (119-131506) may provide an alternative as there is a convenient train service between Hathersage and Edale.
2 Owned by the Peak District National Park Authority, but managed by the Youth Hostels Association. Accommodation is open to all.
3 Situated about ½ mile (800 m) from the Pennine Way.
4 This hostel is 3½ miles (5.5 km) from the Way. Bus or taxi services can be used to reduce this distance.
5 Situated about 1½ miles (2.5 km) from the Pennine Way. There is a bus service from Thornton-in-Craven to Earby.
6 This hostel is situated about 4 miles (6.5 km) from the Way down the B6479. There is a bus service from Horton in Ribblesdale to Stainforth.
7 Situated about ½ mile (800 m) from the Way.
8 Scottish Youth Hostels Association.

It was shown in the 1971 survey that the average walker takes nineteen days to walk the length of the Pennine Way, i.e. an average of nearly 14 miles (22.5 km) per day. On this basis, using Youth Hostels only, there are two stages where excessive distances have to be walked:
(1) Crowden in Longdendale to Mankinholes. Fortunately, this stage may be broken by using the Globe Farm Bunkhouse at Standedge. Although privately owned, this is run on very similar lines to a Youth Hostel and has been open since 1982. Globe Farm, Huddersfield Road, Standedge, Delph, near Oldham. Saddleworth (045 77) 3040.
(2) Byrness to Kirk Yetholm. This stage can only be broken by descending from the ridge soon after Windy Gyle into Upper Coquetdale or the Bowmont Valley, where there is a little accommodation, or by camping/bivouacing along the ridge at some convenient point.

An excellent scheme now available is the Pennine Way Package. The Pennine Way Bureau (see page 174) offers a package of material which includes information on the Way, guide books, maps, hostels, etc. In addition, they will book all accommodation at Youth Hostels for a part/full journey for a small fee.

Hotel, guest and farmhouse accommodation
These vary considerably in quality and price. In themselves they have no particular advantages for Pennine Way travellers, but they may have three disadvantages: (a) they will be more expensive—possibly much more so—than Youth Hostels or camping (b) they may tend to cater more for the tourist trade in general than for walkers in particular (c) most will be small compared to Youth Hostels, possibly necessitating several enquiries to obtain accommodation.

Camping and Bunkhouse Barns
Camping Barns ('stone tents') are usually converted barns which offer shelter and areas for cooking/sleeping. Bunkhouse Barns are similar to simple Youth Hostels, offering self-catering facilities, washing facilities, bunks, etc., although the arrangements vary. Only a few exist at present, but it is likely that the number will increase considerably in the future and acquire greater importance to walkers on the Way.

Camping
Two advantages of camping are: (a) its cheapness once the equipment has been purchased (b) its flexibility, as the walker is not tied to hostels or villages. However, there are several disadvantages: (a) extra weight has to be carried (b) there will be extra tasks in erecting/striking tents, etc. each day (c) supplies will have to be picked up along the way and this will require careful watch on early closing days and on times of arrival, (d) camping is enjoyable in fine weather, but not so much fun in wet weather.

It should be remembered that the Way crosses private land throughout its length and that camping is not a right in such areas. It is safest, therefore, to use a recognized camp-site or to ask a landowner for permission to camp.

Support vehicles (caravans or motorized caravans)
This method is used by some walkers but is dependent, of course, upon having kind friends or relatives who can provide the support and rendezvous with the walking party at the end of each day. Not many walkers will be so lucky!

Sources of information
(a) *The Pennine Way Accommodation and Camping Guide,* Editor John Needham, the Pennine Way Council. This lists all types of accommodation in the area.
(b) *The Rambler's Yearbook,* The Ramblers' Association.
(c) *Farm Pitch Directory List and Long Distance Footpaths List,* The Backpackers Club.
(d) The Camping and Caravanning Club publishes a list of camp-sites either owned by it or run in conjunction with local authorities.
(e) The Tourist Boards whose areas are crossed by the Pennine Way will provide information either directly or through their local Tourist Information Centres. The latter are particularly useful as the staff have local knowledge. Some of these Centres are on the Way and may operate a local Bed-Booking Service or a Book-a-Bed-Ahead Service to personal callers. An excellent guide to these is *Tourist Information Centres in Britain,* English Tourist Board (see also page 174).
(f) *YHA Accommodation Guide: England & Wales,* Youth Hostels Association (England and Wales). Gives full information on all Youth Hostels.
(g) Many farmers along the Way will permit camping on their land, but permission should always be obtained beforehand and the site should be left clean and tidy.

Pre-booking of accommodation can lead to problems if difficulties such as injury or exhaustion occur on the route. During the summer months, however, all accommodation in some of the more popular areas may already be reserved some time before and pre-booking is nearly always essential.

Guides and Books on the Way

(1) Binns, A. P., *Walking the Pennine Way* (Frederick Warne)

(2) Bogg, P., *Laughs along the Pennine Way* (Cicerone)

(3) de Waal, Gerard C., *Going Dutch: The Pennine Way* (Gédéwé)

(4) Hardy, G., *North to south along the Pennine Way* (Frederick Warne)

(5) Haworth, J. (Ed), *The Pennine Way and walks in Derbyshire* (Derbyshire Countryside)

(6) Hopkins, T., *Pennine Way North* and *Pennine Way South* (Aurum Press/Countryside Commission/Ordnance Survey)

(7) Marriott, M., *The Shell Book of the Pennine Way* (The Queen Anne Press)

(8) Oldham, K., *The Pennine Way: Britain's Longest Continuous Footpath* (Dalesman)

(9) Peel, J.H.B., *Along the Pennine Way* (Pan)

(10) Pilton, B., *One Man and His Bog* (Corgi Books)

(11) Stephenson, T., *The Pennine Way* (HMSO)

(12) Wade, H.O., *The Pennine Way in Twenty Days* (Harold Hill)

(13) Wainwright, A., *Pennine Way Companion* (Westmorland Gazette)

(14) Wainwright, A., *Wainwright on the Pennine Way* (Michael Joseph)

(15) Walker, C., *A Walker on the Pennine Way* (Pendyke)

(16) Wood, J., *Mountain Trail: The Pennine Way from the Peak to the Cheviots* (Blackfriars Press)

(17) Wright, C.J., *A Guide to the Pennine Way* (Constable)

(18) *The Pennine Way—Part One, Edale to Teesdale; Part Two, Teesdale to Kirk Yetholm* (Footprint)

In addition to these books a number of pamphlets have been published by the Ramblers' Association, the National Parks Commission, the Countryside Commission, etc. Several books have been published which contain chapters on the Pennine Way.

Maps

(a) Ordnance Survey Landranger 1 : 50 000 (2 cm to 1 km or approx. 1¼ inches to 1 mile)
The full route of the Pennine Way is shown on the following sheets:

74	Kelso
80	Cheviot Hills & Kielder Forest
86	Haltwhistle, Bewcastle & Alston
91	Appleby-in-Westmorland
92	Barnard Castle
98	Wensleydale & Upper Wharfedale
103	Blackburn & Burnley
109	Manchester
110	Sheffield & Huddersfield

(b) Ordnance Survey Outdoor Leisure 1 : 25 000 (4 cm to 1 km or approx. 2½ inches to 1 mile)
These maps give the route in much greater detail than the Landranger series; in particular they show the route in relation to all field boundaries, which is a considerable help in route finding. Unfortunately, however, Outdoor Leisure maps have been published only for the southern part of the Way from Edale to Alston, a distance of about 178 miles (286 km). Furthermore, even within this part, there are two gaps:
(a) North of Black Hill to the crossing of the M62, and (b) Ickornshaw Moor, south of Cowling, to near Gargrave.
The sheets are:
The Peak District—Dark Peak area (No. 1)
South Pennines (No. 21)
Yorkshire Dales—Southern area (No. 10)
Yorkshire Dales—Western area (No. 2)
Yorkshire Dales—Northern & Central areas (No. 30)
Teesdale (No. 31)

(c) Ordnance Survey Pathfinder 1 : 25 000 sheets (4 cm to 1 km or approx. 2½ inches to 1 mile) The Pennine Way is shown on Pathfinder maps, but not on the 1st Series maps which they replaced. Publication of new Pathfinder maps is continuing and is expected to be completed by 1990, except for some areas already covered by Outdoor Leisure sheets.

The following sheets show sections of the Pennine Way:

Pathfinder Sheets: 486 (NT 61/71) Chesters and Howman; 487 (NT 81/91) Cheviot Hills (Central); 475 (NT 82/92) Cheviot Hills (North); 498 (NT 60/70) Catcleugh; 509 (NY 69/79) Kielder; 510 (NY 89/99) Otterburn; 522 (NY 88/98) Bellingham and Kirkwhelpington; 533 (NY 67/77) Wark Forest; 534 (NY 87/97) Wark; 546 (NY 66/76) Haltwhistle and Gilsland; 559 (NY 65/75) Slaggyford; 569 (NY 64/74) Alston; 578 (NY 62/63) Appleby-in-Westmorland; 588 (NY 82/92) Middleton-in-Teesdale; 598 (NY 81/91) North Stainmore and Bowes; 608 (NY80/SD89) Hardrow and Keld; 661 (SD 85/95) Skipton and Hellifield; 670 (SD 84/94) Barnoldswick and Earby; 681 (SD 83/93) Burnley; 701 (SD 81/91) Bury, Rochdale and Littleborough; 702 (SE 01/11) Huddersfield and Marsden; 714 (SE 00/10) Holmfirth and Saddleworth Moor.

Transport in the Pennines

Buses

The 1985 Transport Act, which became operative on 26 October 1986, brought about considerable changes in the overall pattern of bus transport in this country. Deregulation allows anyone who holds an operator's licence to run a bus on any route, at any time and at whatever price he or she wishes, subject only to giving forty-two days' notice of such arrangements. This service may be modified, withdrawn or reintroduced as the operator wishes, subject only to the same period of notice. Local authorities, however, can pay for extra services if they identify gaps in the network where a social need exists. A further development was the breaking up of the state-owned National Bus Company into seventy-three private companies.

It is too early to give a final verdict on these changes, but it seems that bus services have increased in some areas and deteriorated in others. Moreover, it is clear that at present services do change frequently and at short notice and that it is difficult for the general public to obtain information locally on the services that are on offer.

Fortunately, the vast majority of counties have set up enquiry offices which provide information on the services available within their area. For the area of the Pennine Way information may be obtained as follows:

Derbyshire	Matlock (0629) 580000
West Yorkshire	Wakefield (0924) 375555
North Yorkshire	Northallerton (0609) 780780
Durham	Tyneside (091) 386 4411
Cumbria	Carlisle (0228) 23456
Northumberland	Morpeth (0670) 514343
Borders	St. Boswells (0835) 23301

Most of these enquiry offices operate during normal office hours, Monday to Friday. Information may also be obtained from Tourist Information Centres.

Day walkers may find some of 'all-in' tickets, which enable the traveller to use the buses over a wide area, particularly attractive and should make enquiries to ascertain if they are available in the area that they intend to walk. There may also be special walkers' buses. Walkers who finish at Kirk Yetholm may obtain information on bus services from the Borders enquiry office given above. At the present time buses run each day from Kirk Yetholm to Kelso; from there further buses go to Hawick, Berwick and Edinburgh.

From 10th June to 10th September inclusive two special services operate which are of great value to Pennine Way walkers:
(1). The TPT Sherpa Service. Available at Youth Hostels and other accommodation along the Way; rucksacks and walkers can be transported from point to point in a north direction.
(2). The TPT Pennine Way Express. This provides a fast daily minibus service from Kirk Yetholm to Edale calling at Newcastle, Leeds, Sheffield and Manchester as required.

Further information on these two services is available from Trans-Pennine Transport (see page 175).

Trains
The starting point of the Pennine Way at Edale can be reached by train from either Manchester or Sheffield; Edale station is less than ½ mile (800 m) from the start.
Travelling northwards, convenient access points for railway stations are:

ACCESS POINT	STATION
A57, Snake Road	Glossop
Crowden, A628	Hadfield
Mossley-Holmfirth road, A635	Greenfield
Standedge, A62	Marsden
Littleborough-Ripponden road, A58	Littleborough
Calder Valley, A646	Todmorden, Hebden Bridge
Cowling, A6068	Colne, Keighley
Thornton-in-Craven, A56	Skipton
Gargrave, A65	Gargrave
Horton in Ribblesdale, B6479	Settle
Dufton	Appleby
Greenhead, A69	Haltwhistle

Information on train services may be obtained from the following principal stations:

Manchester	(061) 832 8353
Sheffield	(0742) 726411
Huddersfield	(0484) 531226
Bradford	(0274) 733994
Leeds	(0532) 448133
Carlisle	(0228) 44711
Newcastle	(091) 2326262

The Pennine Way Accommodation and Camping Guide includes information on transport.

Alternative Itineraries

According to the 1971 survey (see page 162) the average time taken by walkers to complete the entire length of the Pennine Way was nineteen days and this was used as the basis of the main route description. Some variations on this itinerary are suggested below.

(a) *A journey of two weeks*
The 1971 survey showed that 31% of walkers were taking fifteen days or less over the journey. The following itinerary could be used for a journey of two weeks:

Day	1	Edale to Crowden in Londendale (15 miles/24 km)
	2	Crowden to the Calder Valley (or Mankinholes) (25 miles/40 km)
	3	Calder Valley to Thornton-in-Craven (or Earby) (24 miles/38 km)
	4	Thornton-in-Craven to Malham (11 miles/18 km)
	5	Malham to Horton in Ribblesdale (15 miles/24 km)
	6	Horton in Ribblesdale to Hawes (14 miles/23 km)
	7	Hawes to Keld (13 miles/21 km)
	8	Keld to Middleton-in-Teesdale (21 miles/34 km)
	9	Middleton-in-Teesdale to Dufton (20 miles/32 km)
	10	Dufton to Alston (20 miles/32 km)
	11	Alston to Twice Brewed (25 miles/40 km)

12   Twice Brewed to Bellingham (16 mile/ 26 km)

13   Bellingham to Byrness (15 miles/24 km)

14   Byrness to Kirk Yetholm (28 miles/45 km)

The particularly hard days would be 2, 3, 8, 9, 10, 11 and 14.

(b) *Longer than nineteen days*
Very few walkers (6% in the survey) took longer than twenty-two days. Comparing this to the itinerary of nineteen days, one option is to take three days instead of two over the section from Dufton to Greenhead.

Apart from this it is perhaps better to introduce 'rest days' into the schedule, rather than reduce the average day's walking further. Some suggestions for 'rest points' are given below,

with an indication of the main local attractions:
Calder Valley Heptonstall, Todmorden (History Trail, clog factory), Hebden Dale, cruising on Rochdale Canal.
Ponden Hall Haworth (Brontë Parsonage, Brontë waterfall and bridge, Keighley and Worth Valley Railway, Penistone Hill Country Park).
Malham Janet's Foss, Gordale Scar, National Park Information Centre.
Hawes Town Trail, Rope Works, Upper Dales Folk Museum, National Park Information Centre, Gayle, Hardraw Force.
Bowes Castle and Roman fort, Barnard Castle (Bowes Museum, castle, Egglestone Abbey, Abbey Gorge).
Middleton-in-Teesdale Teesdale, Bowlees Visitor Centre, Gibson's Cave.
Alston South Tynedale Railway.
Bellingham Hareshaw Linn, St Cuthbert's Church.

Safety

About 80% of the Pennine Way crosses moorland or semi-moorland over 1000 ft (305 m) in height. Only 25%, however, is over 1500 ft (457 m) and very little is over 2000 ft (610 m). In the main, therefore, the Way is a high-level moorland walk, although there are some stretches of more gentle country (Aire Gap, Teesdale, South Tyne Valley) and some harsher stretches (Dark Peak, Cross Fell, Cheviot Hills).

In the main the safety aspects of walking the Pennine Way are those which apply to walking in any mountain or moorland area in Britain, with perhaps one proviso: the effect of walking with a full pack, day after day, in good weather or bad, should not be underestimated. The fit, well-prepared, well-equipped, well-organized walker should improve as the walk progresses and should expect to finish fitter than when he or she started. Fitness, preparation and organization are the keys to success on the Pennine Way. It is not a sound

policy to neglect these and hope that everything will be all right on the day.

The general rules for safety in mountain and moorland areas are:

ALWAYS
Carry appropriate clothing and equipment, which should be in a sound condition.
Carry suitable maps (preferably in addition to a guide) and a compass. And know how to use them!
Carry some food and clothing for emergency use, bivouac bag (or similar), whistle, First Aid kit and a torch.
Keep warm, but not over-hot, at all times.
East nourishing foods and rest at regular intervals.
Avoid becoming exhausted.
Know First Aid and the correct procedure in the case of an accident or illness.
Obtain a weather forecast before you set out if

your route crosses particularly wild and rough sections. Watch the weather during the day and take appropriate action if it deteriorates.

NEVER

Attempt the Way on your own, unless you are very experienced.

Leave any member of your party behind on a mountain or moor unless help has to be summoned.

Explore old mine workings (e.g. levels or shafts), quarries or caves.

Attempt to climb rock faces.

Enter any military training areas over which there is no access or public right-of-way.

It is usually recommended that walkers leave a note of their intended route with another person whom they can notify when they return. In practice this is not easy on the Pennine Way as different accommodation is used every night. But it can be done by arranging, for example, to telephone home each evening after reaching accommodation or by coming to some mutual checking arrangement with another party walking up the Way and using the same accommodation. *Make sure, however, that you keep to your arrangements and notify people of your safe arrival so that an alarm is not raised unnecessarily.*

Weather forecasts are sometimes displayed in Youth Hostels, but in any case they can be obtained by telephone (24 hours a day, seven days a week) from Weathercall by dialling 0898 500 followed by:

East Midlands	412
North-west England	416
W & S Yorkshire and Yorkshire Dales	417
North-east England	418
Cumbria & Lake District	419
Borders	422

FINALLY, FOR THE SAFETY OF THE ENVIRONMENT, FOLLOW THE COUNTRY CODE.

Addresses of Useful Organizations

Backpackers Club,
Eric Gurney, Post Box 381,
7–10 Friar Street,
Reading,
Berkshire RG3 4RL
Rotherfield (04917) 739.

Camping and Caravanning Club Ltd.,
11 Lower Grosvenor Place,
London SW1W 0EY
01-828 1012.

English Tourist Board,
Thames Tower,
Black's Road,
Hammersmith,
London W6 9EL
01-730 3400.

HF Holidays Ltd.,
142–144 Great North Way,
Hendon,
London NW4 1EG
01-203 3381. (Guided walks up the Way)

Long Distance Walkers Association,
Membership Secretary,
Kevin Uzzell,
7 Ford Drive,
Yarnfield,
Stone,
Staffordshire
ST15 0RP
Stafford (0785) 760684.

Northumberland National Park and Countryside Department,
Eastburn,
South Park,
Hexham,
Northumberland
NE46 1BS
Hexham (0434) 605555.

P & R Publicity Limited,
Stem Lane Industrial Estate,
Queensway,
New Milton,
Hampshire BH25 5NN
New Milton (0425) 611911. (Pennine Way badge)

Peak Park Joint Planning Board,
Aldern House,
Baslow Road,
Bakewell,
Derbyshire DE4 1AE
Bakewell (062 981) 4321.

Pennine Way Bureau,
c/o YHA Yorkshire Area Office,
96 Main Street,
Bingley
West Yorkshire BD16 2JH
Bingley (0274) 567697. (Pennine Way Package)

Pennine Way Council,
C.D.J. Sainty,
29 Springfield Park Avenue,
Chelmsford,
Essex CM2 6EL
Chelmsford (0245) 256772.
(An organization concerned with the protection of the Way;
individuals may join as Associate Members)

Rambler's Association,
1/5 Wandsworth Road,
London SW8 2XX
01-582 6878.

Scottish Youth Hostels Association,
7 Glebe Crescent,
Stirling,
Scotland FK8 2JA
Stirling (0786) 51181.

Trans-Pennine Transport,
3/25 Cathcart Hill,
London N19 5QN
Telephone enquiries during period of operation is
Grassington (0756) 753146.
(Pennine Way Express and Sherpa services)

Tourist Boards:
Cumbria Tourist Board,
Ashleigh,
Holly Road,
Windermere,
Cumbria LA23 2AS
Windermere (096 62) 4444. (Dufton-Alston section)

East Midlands Tourist Board,
Exchequergate,
Lincoln LN2 1PZ
Lincoln (0522) 531521. (Edale to Black Hill)

Northumbria Tourist Board,
Aykley Heads,
Durham DH1 5UX
Durham (091) 384 6905. (Tan Hill Inn to Langdon Beck and
Alston to the final England-Scotland border crossing)

North West Tourist Board,
The Last Drop Village,
Bromley Cross,
Bolton,
Lancashire BL7 9PZ
Bolton (0204) 591511. (Black Hill to the A58)

Scottish Tourist Board,
23 Ravelston Terrace,
Edinburgh EH4 3EU
Edinburgh (031) 332 2433. (Final section after the border
crossing)

Yorkshire and Humberside Tourist Board,
312 Tadcaster Road,
York YO2 2HF
York (0904) 707961. (Black Hill to Tan Hill Inn)

Yorkshire Dales National Park Committee,
Colvend,
Hebden Road,
Grassington,
Skipton,
North Yorkshire BD23 5LB
Grassington (0756) 752748.

Youth Hostels Association (England and Wales),
Trevelyan House,
8 St Stephen's Hill,
St Albans,
Hertfordshire AL1 2DY
St Albans (0727) 55215.

INDEX

Page numbers in *italics* refer to illustrations.